THE KING
AND THE *Kingdom*

DR JERRY HORNER

ISBN: 978-981-18-9009-3

Published by
ICM Leadership Solutions Pte Ltd
81 UBI AVENUE 4, #11-09,
S(408830)

ENDORSEMENT

Dr. Jerry Horner has been my admired friend and colleague for many years. Former Dean of the Oral Roberts University College of Theology and Ministry and Founding Dean of the Regent University School of Divinity, two of America's premier Christian universities of the twentieth and twenty-first centuries, he is well known and loved by the conservative Christian community everywhere.

This book is the most recent of several other significant works from his hand. However, Jerry has saved the best for now. This book on the Kingdom from this mature scholar-preacher and spiritual statesman is a classic work on the core of the Gospel of our Lord Jesus Christ.

He writes, "God's plan is implicit in the phrase 'the Kingdom of God'. Anyone who misses the significance of that phrase misses the significance of the mission of Jesus Christ on this earth. A gospel of Jesus Christ without the Kingdom of God is not the gospel."

This statement shows the conviction of this esteemed teacher and the central focus of this magnificent book.

I am honored to write this endorsement of such a timely and much-needed book. I recommend it with enthusiasm to every thinking believer in Christ and to every skeptic who has not yet heard the true essence of Jesus' message of God's love, eternal purpose, and gracious provision for us.

Ronald E. Cottle, Ph.D., Ed. D.
Founder and President Emeritus, Christian Life School of Theology Global
September, 2023

Seeking first the Kingdom has absolutely led to God's best in my life. It was a blessing that my former professor from Oral Robert's University, who has also been a family friend and advisor for many years, has shared his depth of wisdom in this great book. In reading this, you will be able to receive the benefit of his many years of study and teaching. You don't need a theology degree to understand what he has written with simplicity and clarity. All you need is a mind ready to receive sound instruction, a heart open to the enlightenment of the Holy Spirit, and a willingness to obey the admonition of the Lord Jesus Christ to seek first the Kingdom of God and His righteousness. This book will guide you in the right direction.

Rachel Plakon
Representative, Florida State Legislature

TABLE OF CONTENTS

INTRODUCTION

In the first words that he writes, the gospel writer Mark tells us the subject about which he is writing: "The beginning of the gospel of Jesus Christ." Then after an essential preliminary concerning the role of John the Baptist in the proclamation of that subject, he writes a momentous statement that summarizes the whole message that he is going to share: "Now after John was put in prison, Jesus came to Galilee, preaching the gospel of the kingdom of God, and saying, 'The time is fulfilled, and the kingdom of God is at hand. Repent, and believe in the gospel'" (Mark 1:14-15). This statement summarizes the whole message that he is going to present in his Gospel. If we want to understand the message and the ministry of Jesus, including His death and resurrection, then we must understand what He taught about the Kingdom of God.

I single out the statement of Jesus in Mark 1:14-15 because it offers a perfect summary of what Christianity stands for and what the gospel message really is. There is no gospel without the Kingdom of God. The New Testament tells us 14 times that Jesus and the early disciples proclaimed the *gospel of the kingdom*. Twice Jesus explicitly stated that the gospel of the Kingdom was the reason He was preaching (Luke 4:43; John 18:37). He left no doubt that the gospel of the Kingdom was not merely a contributory part of His overall message, but the essence of His message. Sad to say, but in this modern age we need more than ever a simple, direct, straightforward statement concerning the essence of the gospel. It's understandable that, since the gospel is many-sided and has many aspects, there have always been certain points, certain facets of truth about which there may be differences of opinion. But it's incredible that so many people, with an open Bible before them, can be wrong about the gospel—wrong about its foundation, wrong about its central message, wrong about its objectives, wrong about the way to embrace it in order to enter a relationship with Jesus Christ. Yet, that's precisely the situation today in a compromising, politically correct society that wants to please everybody, offend nobody, and include everybody.

The unbelieving world is not to blame for this bewilderment. It's the people-pleasing Church that is responsible for the confusion, unwilling to take the risk of being labeled intolerant, narrow-minded, bigoted, and legalistic. So, they preach a soupy, watered-down, feel-good gospel that embraces everyone and is totally devoid of biblical teachings concerning sin, judgment, repentance, and the demand for holiness and absolute surrender to the lordship of Jesus Christ. Some even argue that the Bible is outdated and has little relevance to this modern age, so we need to modernize the Christian message to accommodate a diverse and advanced society and thus improve the world's condition. "The Church has no hope of reaching modern civilization," they say, "because people are now different. They know things they didn't know a hundred years ago."

People of this persuasion would have us believe that the message of Jesus was a simple philosophy of love, and He served as a living example that we should all love one another. He taught a message about the fundamental brotherhood of mankind—that God is our Father and that all people are brothers and sisters under Him. His message included tolerance and respect for others, exemplified by the fact that

He didn't go around condemning people or judging them; but that He accepted them and welcomed them for who they were. His message was about justice and equality. His was a truly "social gospel," for He taught that we should care for the poor and needy, do what we can to alleviate the suffering in the world, and demand that the rich and the privileged should give of their wealth to meet the needs of others. He even called upon His followers to love their enemies (Matthew 5:44; Luke 6:27). Jesus said that loving God is the greatest commandment, and loving our neighbors is a close second (Mark 12:29-31).

While love was a prominent topic in the message of Jesus, it was not the core of His proclamation. If Jesus had been traversing first-century Judea calling on people to love each other, He doubtless would never have been crucified on a Roman cross. At worst, most Jews would have scorned a so-called prophet who told them to love each other, never mind their enemies. And the Romans, who were the obvious enemies of first-century Jews, wouldn't have crucified someone charged with the crime of telling Jews to love them and to turn the other cheek. On the contrary, the Romans would surely have protected a peacemaker who preached such a message. The message of Jesus was more than a call to love. It was something so extremely contentious that it angered the religious leaders to the extent that it got Him killed on a Roman cross.

In reality, the contemporary limitation of the message of Jesus is the enterprise of preachers who change His basic message into mere expressions of their own beliefs and biases. They project their own values and priorities onto Jesus and present Him as the great teacher of the things that they believe the public wants to hear. To restrict the gospel message in such a way is absolute nonsense because it ignores two basic facts. One is that God is still the same as He always has been. God does not change, and intellectual, cultural, sociological, scientific advancements, or any other kind of developments in civilization, make not the slightest difference to Him. God's righteous and holy character is always what He has revealed it to be. It is impossible that He will ever change. He is "the Father of lights, with whom there is no variation or shadow of turning" (James 1:17). "From everlasting to everlasting" He is the eternal absolute God (Psalm 90:2).

Those who want to update the gospel also ignore the fact that people have not changed. The tremendous advances in civilization make no difference in the morality of people. They still have the same lusts and passions and evil desires within them. They deal with the same temptations and face the same needs and problems.

Therefore, it is extremely urgent that we be clear about the basic message of Jesus. because if we are wrong about the fundamentals of the gospel, then everything else will be wrong. That fact should be obvious. If you start a journey to an intended destination, you will never arrive there if you set out on the wrong road. Even though we are living in an age of scientific technology that was beyond imagination only a few years ago, we are living in an age of moral and spiritual failure that was also beyond imagination a few years ago. Until recently we had no problem distinguishing between a man and a woman. Now we have a Supreme Court justice who says that she cannot give a definition of a woman, because she is not a biologist.

We are surrounded by utter confusion and despair, baffled by the immensity of the problems confronting us. The efforts of politicians to solve matters through legislation have only made things worse. The dogmatic assertions of environmentalists and the theoretical speculations of philosophers, humanists, sociologists, and psychologists only fuel the atmosphere of utter hopelessness, because they all ignore the fact that the basic problem of mankind is sin. And so, they continue their pursuits for a solution.

However, we don't need to waste a second in trying to discover the solution. Even before time began God had a plan and a purpose for this world to deliver people out of the morass into which they have fallen. The message of the Bible is not that we should try to discover the truth; it is that we should hear and proclaim the truth that God has already revealed. And since God has already given His revelation, the people who first received it knew as much as we know, and nobody will ever know more than they did. If the world lasts another million years, people will never know more about God or about Christ or about salvation than they can know now if they read the Bible with spiritual eyes. God's plan is implicit in the phrase, "the Kingdom of God." Anyone who misses the significance of that phrase misses the significance of the mission of Jesus Christ on this earth. A gospel of Jesus without the Kingdom of God is not the gospel. The Bible presents God as a King who rules over a Kingdom, and that topic is a critical aspect of biblical teaching. Therefore, we need to have a thorough, more comprehensive understanding of what the Bible says about the rule of God and His Kingdom, absolute sovereignty, and absolute free exercise of His will without any consultation or restraint. That's what it means to be king of everything.

I

The Kingdom

EXPECTING THE KINGDOM

Jesus began His ministry by proclaiming that the Kingdom is "at hand" (Matthew 3:2; Mark 1:15). Nothing else He might have said would have captivated the attention of His audience and roused their hopes more forcefully than those few words. His dramatic announcement surely created an electrifying buzz. There may have been skeptics among them, but they all grasped what He was talking about. Even if they had misconceptions of the meaning of the Kingdom of God, the term was very familiar to them, because it had been the foremost and the most passionate expectation of Israel for centuries. They understood that Jesus was telling them that what God had been promising them throughout their history had finally been realized. What was the basis of their expectation? It was their Scriptures. The pages of the document that we know as the Old Testament are replete with references to the Kingdom of God, even though the exact term is not found. The word "king" suggests that there must be a kingdom over which to reign, and throughout the Old Testament the sovereign rule of God is proclaimed and celebrated. We cannot gain an adequate understanding of the preaching of Jesus about the Kingdom of God without first seeking an understanding of what the Old Testament has to say about it.

God Possesses Absolute Sovereignty

We tend to think of the words "king" and "kingdom" in an earthly territorial sense, or perhaps in the negative sense of a dictator with oppressive absolute power. Those of us who have never experienced living under an absolute monarchy know only the sovereignty of the populace, with a balance of power spread out over many elected officials and agencies in a kind of check and balance system. It's the very antithesis of a monarchy, a system in which no one is supreme, possessing absolute rights, privilege, power, and authority. Consequently, we have difficulty understanding the concept of absolute supremacy and unassailable rights. But that's exactly what God claims for Himself—absolute sovereignty, absolute free exercise of His will without any consultation or restraint. That's what it means to be king of everything. God's rule is explicitly described as everlasting: "Your kingdom is an everlasting kingdom, and Your dominion endures throughout all generations" (Psalm 145:13). "The Lord sits as King forever" (Psalm 29:10). His sovereignty is universal: "The Lord has established His throne in heaven, and His kingdom rules over all" (Psalm 103:19).

Throughout its entirety, the Old Testament proclaims the truth of the absolute supremacy and sovereignty of God. The Kingdom of God is the rule of God, and the whole Bible declares that God is King. As the Creator, He is both King of nature (sustaining what He has made) and King of history (ordering the life of nations). "The Lord reigns" is a frequent shout of joy in the Old Testament, expressing Israel's confidence in the providential rule of God over the world. Notice only a few passages. Isaiah 40:12 asks these rhetorical questions: " Who has measured the waters in the hollow of His hand, measured heaven with a span and calculated the dust of the earth in a measure? Weighed the mountains in scales and the hills in a balance?" In other words, who is equal to God? What counselor has given advice or information to God? Who instructed God in the way of justice and understanding? The only answer to every one of those questions is nobody. Because of His absolute perfection, His perfect knowledge, His perfect wisdom, His perfect power, and His perfect will, God does precisely what He wants, when He wants, with whom He wants, and for the purpose He wants.

Job understood this truth: "I know that You can do everything, and that no purpose of Yours can be withheld from You" (Job 42:2). Isaiah 14:27 affirms, "For the Lord of hosts has purposed, and who will annul it? His hand is stretched out, and who will turn it back?" God is sovereign. He establishes His purposes and makes His plans to do what He wants, and He does exactly that. Nobody can change or frustrate that which God purposes. God says in Isaiah 46:8-11: "Remember this, and show yourselves men; recall to mind, O you transgressors. Remember the former things of old, for I am God, and there is no other; I am God, and there is none like Me, declaring the end from the beginning, and from ancient times things that are not yet done, saying, 'My counsel shall stand, and I will do all My pleasure,' calling a bird of prey from the east, the man who executes My counsel, from a far country. Indeed I have spoken it; I will also bring it to pass. I have purposed it; I will also do it." God calls upon the people to clear up their normally sin-stained thinking in order to think accurately about Him.

In Romans 11:33-36 the apostle Paul sums up these teachings found in Isaiah and Job: "Oh, the depth of the riches both of the wisdom and knowledge of God! How unsearchable are His judgments and His ways past finding out! For who has known the mind of the Lord? Or who has become His counselor? Or who has first given to Him and it shall be repaid to Him? For of Him and through Him and to Him are all things, to whom be glory forever. Amen." This passage tells us that God has supreme wisdom and knowledge, and He makes supreme judgments based on information that is not available to us. It is unsearchable. And we cannot understand what God does, because His ways are unfathomable. Nobody has given Him counsel, nor has He asked the advice from anyone. Nor has anyone done anything for God that would incur His obligation to pay him back. God is unreservedly supreme and sovereign.

David was aware of the absolute sovereignty of God when he extolled Him before the assembly: "Blessed are You, Lord God of Israel, our Father, forever and ever. Yours, O Lord, is the greatness, the power and the glory, the victory and the majesty; for all that is in heaven and in earth is Yours; Yours is the kingdom, O Lord, and You are exalted as head over all. Both riches and honor come from You, and You reign over all. In Your hand is power and might; in Your hand it is to make great and to give strength to all. Now therefore, our God, we thank You And praise Your glorious name" (1 Chronicles 29:11-13).

God Is King Over Creation

The most important teaching on the Kingdom in the Old Testament is that God is King, and that teaching begins with the story of creation. Genesis 1 was not written to give us a scientific explanation of the origin of the earth. We're missing the point when we argue about the age of the earth in Genesis 1, because it's much more significant that God is revealing Himself to be the King who rules over all creation, a fact that the Old Testament makes abundantly clear. Psalm 10:16 says, "The Lord *is* King forever and ever; the nations have perished out of His land." King Jehoshaphat confesses in 2 Chronicles 20:6: "O Lord God of our fathers, are You not God in heaven, and do You not rule over all the kingdoms of the nations, and in Your hand is there not power and might, so that no one is able to withstand You?" King Hezekiah exults in Isaiah 37:16: "O

Lord of hosts, God of Israel, the One who dwells between the cherubim, You are God, You alone, of all the kingdoms of the earth. You have made heaven and earth." (See also Psalms 93:1-2; 95:3-6; 96:10; 104; 136:1-9.) God is the sovereign ruler, the King, of the universe that He created. Every molecule, every atom, and every component of an atom belongs in His kingdom. God is sovereign over the material universe because He created it and because He controls it. If God created the furthest star, God is sovereign over that star. God is in control of that star. God is the Lord of that star. If God creates a blade of grass, He owns it, although we may think we own it because it's on our property. God is the one who creates everything everywhere, and therefore the Bible reveals that because God created everything everywhere, God owns everything everywhere. To put it simply, God is the Lord of everything everywhere. God is the master of everything everywhere.

The Universe

Consider first the infinite vastness of the universe. Psalm 19:1 declares, "The heavens declare the glory of God; and the firmament shows His handiwork." Scientists are always trying to discover the mystery of the universe. They sent out space probes and the Hubble telescope to collect all kinds of data and thought they learned a lot. Then they sent out the Webb telescope, which is a hundred times more powerful than the Hubble, and they found out that they didn't know a lot of things that they thought they knew. Every new discovery makes it more difficult to explain creation apart from the simple opening statement of the Bible: "In the beginning God created the heavens and the earth" (Genesis 1:1). You must possess enormous faith these days to be an evolutionist or atheist and believe all this happened randomly after some big bang and swirling chaos of explosions and lucky naturalism finally worked things out just right and perfectly. The Bible says that the person who says there is no God is a fool (Psalm 14:1). The word "fool" doesn't mean idiot or ignoramus or intellectually deficient, but someone with a moral problem who suppresses God's truth and has no spiritual understanding.

The seventeenth-century mathematician and physicist Sir Isaac Newton had a skillful mechanic to make him a replica of our solar system in miniature. In the center was a large, gilded ball representing the sun, and revolving in the proper order around it were smaller spheres fixed on the ends of rods of varying lengths, representing the planets. These bails were geared together by cogs and belts to make them move around the sun in perfect harmony when turned by a crank. One day, as Newton sat reading in his study with his mechanism on a large table near him, a scientist friend stepped in. Newton was a devout Christian and an ardent student of the Bible, but the friend was an infidel. Recognizing the device as a model of the solar system, the unbelieving scientist went over to it and slowly turned the crank. He marveled with laudatory admiration as he watched the heavenly bodies all move at their relative speeds in their orbits. With amazement, he exclaimed, "What an exquisite thing this is! Who made it?"

Newton nonchalantly answered, "Nobody!"

The friend responded, "Evidently you did not understand my question. I asked who made this?" Newton solemnly assured him that nobody made it, explaining that all those balls and cogs and belts and gears just happened to come together, and wonder of wonders, by chance they began revolving in their set orbits and with perfect timing. But the astonished infidel replied with some exasperation, "You must think I am a fool! Somebody had to make this device, and he's a genius."

Newton answered, "This thing is just a puny imitation of our great solar system, whose laws you know. I'm not able to convince you that this mere toy is without a design and maker, yet you profess to believe that the great original from which the design is taken has come into being without either designer or maker! Now tell me by what sort of reasoning do you reach such an incongruous conclusion?" The unbelieving friend got the point.

We are all amazed at the vastness of our solar system, but actually, it's quite tiny. It consists of just nine planets, and they have a total of 28 moons and some little planetoids flying around them. All these planets and their moons are orbiting around the sun, which is 93 million miles from Earth. But all of this is just an infinitesimal speck in God's great universe. In comparison to other heavenly bodies, Earth is just a pinprick that can hardly be noticed. For example, Jupiter is 1,300 times bigger than Earth, and that's just in our minute solar system, which is in the outer spiral arm of the galaxy known as the Milky Way. There are from 200 to 400 million stars in our galaxy, and some of those stars are more than 300 million miles across. That's three times the distance from Earth to the sun, and there are millions of those stars!

Let me try to illustrate how great. God's universe is. There are more suns in the universe than there are grains of sand in all the seashores on Earth. Go to the nearest beach, scoop up a handful of sand, and start counting. How many grains of sand are there in a square foot? Can you imagine how many there are on all the beaches on Earth? There are more suns than that just in our galaxy, and in the observable universe, there are more than 170 billion suns, with hundreds of billions of stars. But even these statistics are small in comparison to a recent discovery. Scientists found a hole in one of the outermost parts of the universe, the size of a speck held at arm's length. They trained the powerful Webb telescope on it and left the lens open for a long period of time. When they developed the picture that was taken in that tiny hole, they discovered more than 1,500 previously unknown galaxies. Not stars! Not solar systems! Galaxies! One expert was so staggered that he exclaimed that there are more stars in the universe than there are words and sounds that all humans of all time have ever spoken.

Let's use the speed of light, which is 186,000 miles a second, to illustrate the vastness of the universe. The closest complete galaxy to our own that is observable to the naked eye is called Andromeda. It appears as a faint speck in the sky, more than two and a half million light years away. How far is a light year? A light year is how far light travels in a year at the rate of 186,000 miles a second. How fast is that? If I were to strike a match, the light produced would go around the world before I could blow it out. It's that fast, and light from Andromeda has been traveling more than two and a half million years at that speed, that is, unless God already created it in progress, which I believe He did.

This is the grand, universal, external kingdom of God by which He rules sovereignly over everything that He has made. But according to Psalm 8:3, however big this seemingly immense and immeasurable and incalculably vast universe is, it's just fingerwork for God. Isaiah 40:12 says that the universe can fit into the span of God's hand. He made it all. You can see the rule of God in His universal Kingdom by just looking out there. Someone may ask, "If Earth is the only inhabited planet and man the only rational inhabitant among the stars, why such a large and empty universe?" The crystal-clear answer is found in Psalm 19:1: "The heavens declare the glory of God," and the reason we exist is to see it and be stunned by it and glorify God because of it. The splendor of the universe is a breathtaking exhibition of the glory of God, and according to Romans 1:20-21, it leaves without excuse everybody on the planet who doesn't see God and His massive power and wisdom in the creation. God has revealed Himself in that creation. So, He is the King who has manifested Himself. There is a natural revelation in human reason and in the moral law written in the heart and the conscience that makes every individual responsible for the knowledge of God as King over His created universe.

There was a king by the name of Nebuchadnezzar who thought that he could compete with the sovereign of the universe. For attempting to steal the glory from God, he ended up as a raving maniac for seven years living like an animal. At the end of that period, when he finally came to his senses, he said, "I, Nebuchadnezzar, lifted my eyes to heaven and my understanding returned to me" (Daniel 4:34). This is the position of all reasonable people. If you're truly reasonable, you're going to express the same awe that Nebuchadnezzar felt when he said: "I blessed the Most High, and praised and honored Him who lives forever. For His dominion is an everlasting dominion, His kingdom is from generation to generation. All the inhabitants of the earth are reputed as nothing; He does according to His will in the army of heaven and among the inhabitants of earth. No one can restrain His hand or say to Him, 'What have you done?' At that same time, my reason returned to me and for the glory of my kingdom, my honor and splendor returned to me. My counselors and nobles resorted to me. I was restored to my kingdom, and excellent majesty was added to me. Now I, Nebuchadnezzar, praise, extol and honor the King of heaven, all whose works are truth, and His ways justice. And those who walk in pride He is able to put down" (Daniel 4:34-36).

But let's leave the vastness of the universe and consider the smallness of Earth.

The Earth

God's sovereignty over the universe includes Earth, especially since He created this planet for a special purpose. The question is not whether God owns us or not; the question is whether we recognize His ownership or not. The apostle Paul gave a clear and convincing commentary on Genesis 1:1 in his speech recorded in Acts 17:22-31. He was not in a Jewish synagogue in Jerusalem. He was in Athens, addressing a group of Greek philosophers who knew nothing about the Jewish God or the Jewish Scriptures. So, he began with what they did know by observation. He first exposed the fallacy of their worship of idols, and then he pointed them to the true God "who made the world and everything in it." Because God is the creator, "He is Lord of heaven and earth," and they are subject to Him.

Out of the hundreds of billions of heavenly bodies, God chose only one to be inhabited, and He designed it perfectly for life, down to the most minute detail. Consider, for example, some facts about God's design of the atmosphere in which we live. Scientists have proved that 21% oxygen is exactly the right amount. If it were 25%, fires would erupt; if 15%, human beings would suffocate. In addition, God designed the atmosphere to have precise levels of water vapors. The experts tell us that if water vapor levels in the atmosphere were greater than they are now, a runaway greenhouse effect would cause temperatures to rise too high for human life, but if they were less, an insufficient greenhouse effect would make the earth too cold to support human life.

God saw to it that just the right level of carbon dioxide is maintained naturally in Earth's atmosphere. If the CO2 level were higher than it is now, the heat would make our life impossible. If the level were lower than it is now, plants would not be able to maintain efficient photosynthesis, and we wouldn't be able to breathe. The right ratio of nitrogen and ozone is also critical for life. Scientists have also shown that the degree of transparency of the atmosphere is essential for life. If the atmosphere were less transparent, not enough solar radiation would reach Earth's surface. If it were more transparent, we would be bombarded with far too much solar radiation down here. God knew exactly what He was doing when He formed the atmosphere.

God created not only the perfect atmosphere for life, but He also created the perfect balance of land masses. Consider the following facts discovered by modern science:

*Earth has the perfect ocean levels and just the right level and percentage of water. Without that exactness, life would be impossible.

*The thickness of the earth's crust is just right to sustain life. A greater thickness, even just ten more feet of solid matter added to the planet's diameter, would result in too much oxygen being transferred to the crust to support life. If it were thinner, volcanic and tectonic activity would make life unsustainable.

*If the 23-degree axial tilt of the earth were altered slightly, life would not be possible.

*The earth has a slight wobble angle of three degrees, and if it were more or less, the planet would not be hospitable, to say the least.

*The planet turns once a day at a rotational speed of 1,000 miles per hour at the equator.
If it rotated slower on its axis, all life would cease to exist, either by freezing at night or by burning heat during the day.

*The diameter of the earth at the equator is 7,926 miles, which is just right for life. A significant difference would cause enormous problems with gravity and other chain reactions.

* Even earthquakes have a part to play in sustaining life as we know it. Greater seismic activity would result in greater loss of life. Less seismic activity would restrict nutrients on the ocean floors and in river runoff from being cycled back to the continents through tectonic uplift.

God is a great artist, and it would be impossible to describe the incredibly beautiful Earth that He painted. This planet is like a beautiful canvas of radiant colors The diversity of God's creation is amazing and completely overwhelming. Biologists have discovered and named a total of between 1.5 million and 1.8 million species of animals, plants, and insects on Earth, but they say those figures represent only a tiny fraction of all the species. Some specialists estimate that the true number of living species is more than 100 million. An amazing example of God's infinite creativity is seen in the 400 billion trees in the Amazon rainforest, an average of 200 trees per acre. The trees belong to over 16,000 known species. A typical 2.5-acre area of the rainforest will contain 750 kinds of trees and 1,500 species of higher plants. In one small corner of Peru's Manu National Park, there are 1,307 butterfly species and more than 1,000 species of birds. These and countless other examples display the creative activity of a great God of awesome wonder and design and incite us to shout, "You are worthy, O Lord, to receive glory and honor; for You created all things, and by Your will they exist and were created" (Revelation 4:11).

The question is, "Why would God single out this one pinpoint in His limitless universe and prepare it as the only perfect spot to sustain life?" God certainly did not create the world because He was lonely, bored, or starving for attention. He did not create out of need. He did not create the world because of a deficiency that needed to be made up. The short answer that resounds through the whole Bible is that God created the world for His glory. The angels cry in Isaiah 6:3, "Holy, holy, holy is the Lord of hosts; the whole earth is full of His glory." The Bible declares that ever since the creation of the world God's invisible attributes, namely, his eternal power and divine nature, have been "clearly seen, being understood by the things that have been made" (Romans 1:20). Isaiah plainly states that we were created for God's glory (Isaiah 43:7; see 40:4-5; 42:8; 44:23; 48:9-11; 60:2).

But the question is not just, "Why did God create the world?" We must ask, "Why did God create *this* world?" Why would God, who is infinitely good and perfectly holy, create a world that would rebel against Him, sink into the abysmal depths of sin, and exchange the glory of God for man-made grotesque images? The brief answer is that God created this kind of world for the glory of His grace displayed supremely in the death of Jesus on the cross. When God created the earth, He was setting the stage for the true drama of history to unfold, which is the drama of salvation, the story of love, loss, separation, and redemption. In a condensed statement, this world exists for the glory of God's grace supremely shown in the saving work of Jesus Christ. According to Ephesians 1:5-6, the glory of God's grace, which Ephesians 2:7 calls "the exceeding riches of His grace in His kindness toward us in Christ Jesus," is the highpoint and endpoint in the revelation of God's glory. Grace is the summit of the mountain of God's glory. And the aim of God's plan is that we live to the praise of the glory of His grace forever. This is why Revelation 5:9-13 proclaims that for all eternity "every creature which is in heaven and on the earth and under the earth and such as are in the sea, and all that are in them," "ten thousand times ten thousand, and thousands and thousands" will sing "the song of the Lamb." With fervent reverberating praise, we will sing: "You are worthy to take the scroll, and to open its seals; for You were slain, and have redeemed us to God by Your blood out of every tribe and tongue and people and nation."

We will never exhaust the list of things for which we will praise our Savior, but we will never say anything more glorious than "You were slain and have redeemed us." Isaiah was privileged to look into heaven, and he "saw the Lord sitting on a throne," and around the throne were angels singing, "Holy, holy, holy . . . " (Isaiah 6:1-3). The hymn writer Johnson Oatman adds to that scene:

> Holy, holy, is what the angels sing,
> And I expect to help them make the courts of Heaven ring;
> But when I sing redemption's story, they will fold their wings,

For angels never felt the joys that our salvation brings.

The amazing thing is that even before He created the world, God formulated this plan of redemption. The stunning statement of Ephesians 1:4-6 tells us that God chose us in Christ *"before the foundation of the world . . . to the praise of the glory of His grace."* Grace was not a desperate last-minute response to the fall of man. It was God's plan from before creation, as clearly stated in such passages as Ephesians 1:4-6, 2 Timothy 1:9, and Revelation 13:8. God had already planned redemption from sin even before sin entered the world. Before there was a tree of life in Eden, there was a tree of death on Calvary.

Humankind

When He created the universe, God said, "Let Us make man in Our image, according to Our likeness; let them have dominion over the fish of the sea and over the birds of the air, and over the cattle, over all the earth and over every creeping thing that creeps on the earth" (Genesis 1:26). Kingship is at the heart of the commission that God gives to Adam. First, God made man and woman in His own image so that human beings are like God as no other earthly creatures are. God created man with a soul or spirit-self-conscious and with a personal God-like capacity for rational intelligence, will, and action. God created man morally upright, to reflect and reproduce His Holy character. God commissioned Adam to have rule or dominion over His creation as a regent or subordinate king underneath God and representing Him, the true King over all. The word "dominion," used twice in the commission given to Adam in Genesis 1:26-30, is exactly what it sounds like. As the one who, uniquely among all created beings, has been created in God's likeness and image, Adam's responsibility was to rule creation. Starting in Eden, he was to spread God's own dominion outside the boundaries of the Garden until the whole world is subdued under his, and therefore God's, rule. In this sense, God reigned over His creation in and through Adam. The title "king" connotes authority, power, and might, all of which Adam was commissioned to exercise on Earth.

For a while, it seemed that man's domain was secure, enjoyable, and prospering. God Himself fellowshipped with His regent, and the kingdom on Earth was doing the will of the kingdom in heaven. It seemed to be a beautiful arrangement in which heaven and Earth met. God was establishing a system of authority wherein man would rule over creation, exercising the authority of the Creator Himself, the Lord, the High King of the universe. But it's important to understand that although God gave Adam and Eve dominion over creation, their rule was not ultimate. God was the High King and they were but His regents. Therefore, their authority and dominion were derived from Him and secondary to His rule. Thus, they were limited by their subjection to God. That subjection is the true meaning of the tree God set in the middle of the garden. The reason He told Adam and Eve that they could not eat the fruit of the tree was to remind them that there was a higher authority and power than their own, a higher ruler who could command and limit them.

That tree, called "the tree of the knowledge of good and evil" in Genesis 2:9, had another purpose as well. God gave Adam instructions "to tend and keep" the garden, that is, to "work" and "guard" it (Genesis 2:15). Adam's responsibility as king in the garden was to protect it, to prevent any evil from entering it. If any impure thing did enter, he was to it and cast it out. In addition to reminding Adam of the limits of his authority, the tree of the knowledge of good and evil was intended to remind him of his responsibility to guard and protect from evil. "To know good and evil," means to discern the difference and judge between them. In the Old Testament, the phrase was commonly used to describe the responsibility of a king. For example, in 2 Samuel 14:17 a woman from the town of Tekoa explains to King David what prompted her to come to him: "The word of my lord the king will now be comforting; for as the angel of God, so is my lord the king in discerning good and evil." We read in 1 Kings 3:9 that when Solomon was about to undertake the burdens of the kingship, he prayed, "Therefore give to Your servant an understanding heart to judge Your people, that I may discern between good and evil. For who is able to judge this great people of Yours?"

The tree of the knowledge of good and evil, therefore, was more than a magical plant that granted great wisdom to people. It was, rather, the judgment seat where King Adam was to exercise discernment between good and evil. However, when the testing time came Adam failed to discern the evil that the serpent represented. Instead of judging it and casting it completely out of the garden, Adam and Eve both allowed their discernment to be so twisted that they followed the serpent's insinuation that God was wrong in that he denied them something that was their right. The deception was that they didn't need God. They can rule without Him. By joining the serpent in his rebellion, they were declaring their independence from the rule of God and His authority over them. By his disastrous action, Adam failed miserably in his responsibility as king, and when he fell, he took the whole world out from under God's good rule and into the realm of darkness and sin. When Adam and Eve succumbed to the temptation of Satan in the garden, they catapulted the whole human race into sin and rebellion, and they came under the kingdom of someone else, whose rule is oppressive and evil. He is called "the ruler of this world" (John 12:31), "the god of this age" (2 Corinthians 4:4), and "the prince of the power of the air" (Ephesians 2:2). So, anyone who is not under the rule of the righteous King is under the rule of an evil tyrant. There is no middle ground.

The rebellious sin in Eden brought a curse that has stained God's material kingdom. The universe is in the process of disintegrating, heading toward the disastrous dissolution described in 2 Peter 3:10: "But the day of the Lord will come as a thief in the night, in which the heavens will pass away with a great noise, and the elements will melt with fervent heat; both the earth and the works that are in it will be burned up." This universe exists groaning under the curse, but the good news, as we have seen, is that immediately after the tragic event in Eden, God promised to overthrow the tyrant. God is still sovereign, and one day He will redeem and restore the paradise that was lost in the garden.

God Is King Over Israel

God did not abandon His intention to rule over the earth through a human king when Adam rebelled against His dominion. His purpose did not waver or change in His avowal to establish a Kingdom in this world. Therefore, all through the Bible, from its beginning to its ending, and without deviation, there is outlined and revealed the purpose of God to build His Kingdom. It all begins in Eden when God utters the first proclamation of the good news of the gospel. He cursed the serpent and said to him: "And I will put enmity between you and the woman, and between your seed and her Seed; He shall bruise your head, and you shall bruise His heel" (Genesis 3:15). That's good news because God promises to send a descendent of Eve to crush the head of the serpent, to defeat Satan's rule. God promises to push Satan out. He has a plan to reestablish His reign, restore His realm, and bring redemption to His fallen subjects. The biblical story from that moment is an unfolding of God's plan and purpose to fulfill His promise. Let's not overlook the significant fact that the good news proclaimed in Genesis 3:15 isn't just the coming of a King. It's the coming of a King who will reverse the death and separation from God that resulted from sin. In other words, the arrival of the King will mean salvation. The King will save.

Under Satan's rule men and women continued to rebel, to the extent that God sent a flood to wipe out all of humanity. After the flood, God started over with Noah, but the effects of sin persisted. God chose a family through which to bring his kingdom and King. He singled out a man named Abram, whom He later renamed Abraham, and God promised that He will bless him by making him the father of a great nation, and God will use his countless descendants to bless the world. The promise is found in Genesis 12:1-3: "Get out of your country, from your family and from your father's house, to a land that I will show you. I will make you a great nation; I will bless you and make your name great; and you shall be a blessing. I will bless those who bless you, and I will curse him who curses you; and in you all the families of the earth shall be blessed." God repeats the promise in Genesis 17:1-8.

God's plan is that He will destroy the prince of this world and restore the kingdom of God on earth. Through Abraham's line, God will form the Hebrew people, and he will use that nation to bring God's reign on earth, the restoration of His realm, and the redemption of His people. We have in the promise to Abraham a preview of what the kingdom of God is. There are three essential features: reign, God reestablishing His presence on earth; realm, God restoring all of creation from the fall; redemption, God redeeming His fallen subjects. Briefly, we can then summarize the kingdom of God as a reign, a realm, and the redeemed.

Fast forward through the history of the Hebrews to where the former slaves are gathered at the foot of Mount Sinai after their deliverance from 400 years of Egyptian captivity. There God identifies them as His chosen nation: "Now therefore, if you will indeed obey My voice and keep My covenant, then you shall be a special treasure to Me above all people; for all the earth is Mine. And you shall be to Me a kingdom of priests and a holy nation" (Exodus 19:5-6). God declares that they would be a special nation with a direct relationship with Him. From that point on, the words "you shall be to Me a kingdom" formed the definitive foundation that set the people of Israel apart as a chosen nation.

But God made it quite clear that it would be a kingdom on His terms, not Israel's. A kingdom must have laws, and at Sinai God gave the laws that govern His Kingdom. The fulfillment of God's plan is contingent upon the will of the people to obey Him fully and keep His law, as indicated by the conditional clause, "If you will indeed obey." Through the succeeding generations of Israel's history, this condition of obedience was the deciding factor in the establishment of God's Kingdom on earth. His Kingdom can't exist on earth unless there is total and complete submission to His will and His purposes and obedience to his commandments. Constantly in the Old Testament God's call to obedience rang out through prophets, priests, and kings. As we shall discover, the New Testament has the same emphasis.

God's Rule and Earthly Kings

So, God has formed His nation. As we found in Exodus 19:6, God intended Israel to be a kingdom of priests, under the rule of God Himself. However, God foresaw that Israel would one day reject Him as their king and demand a king that matched the kings of other nations (1 Samuel 8:7). Therefore, just before Israel crossed into the Promised Land, God gave them a description of the king He desired and guidelines for how the king should rule:

"You shall surely set a king over you whom the Lord your God chooses; one from among your brethren you shall set as king over you; you may not set a foreigner over you, who is not your brother. But he shall not multiply horses for himself, nor cause the people to return to

Egypt to multiply horses, for the Lord has said to you, 'You shall not return that way again.' Neither shall he multiply wives for himself, lest his heart turn away; nor shall he greatly multiply silver and gold for himself" (Deuteronomy17:15-17).

The ruler chosen by God couldn't acquire lots of horses, which meant he couldn't build a big army. He wasn't supposed to lead the people back to Egypt, thinking to find safety, but where instead there was oppression. He was not to marry a lot of women, which was a way to form political alliances, and he should not focus on piling up material treasure. He was to concentrate on governing by the Word of God, as evidenced by the following instructions:

"Also it shall be, when he sits on the throne of his kingdom, that he shall write for himself a copy of this law in a book, from the one before the priests, the Levites. And it shall be with him, and he shall read it all the days of his life, that he may learn to fear the Lord his God and be careful to observe all the words of this law and these statutes" (Deuteronomy 17:18-19). The king was supposed to make for himself a copy of the law, the Scriptures, and he was to read it and meditate on it every day of his life. Only then could he learn to obey the Lord and lead the people in obedience to God.

So, God indeed had a plan to establish His Kingdom, His rulership, on earth, but it must be done with kings of His choosing and in His way and in His time. God intended the king to do what Adam and Eve failed to do—rule justly while being dependent on Him. While these guidelines were intended for the nation of Israel centuries ago, they are still applicable to governments today. The worldly kingdoms that we establish today are vastly different from the Kingdom of God. Instead of concentrating on the laws of God, our nation relies on military might, storehouses of gold, consensus of human opinions, and political alliances. It's highly unlikely that any of our political leaders are hand-copying the Bible for themselves. The lesson that we are to learn thus far from the Old Testament is that while it is true that God alone is the ultimate King of Israel and over all of creation, human kings have a key role to play in God's kingdom. However, they can fulfill that role only when they follow the principles of rulership that God has established.

Once they settled in the land that God had promised them, the nation of Israel rapidly declined spiritually, morally, and politically. Israel was God's people. He was their King. Unfortunately, they failed to resist sinful Canaanite influences and they disregarded the laws that God had mandated. Their disobedience led to idolatry, blatant immorality, and anarchy. The condition of the nation during this period of turbulence is summed up in the pathetic words of Judges 21:25: "In those days there was no king in Israel; everyone did what was right in his own eyes." During this political and religious turmoil, the people clamored for a centralized monarchy, thinking that it would bring stability to the people. But what they wanted was not what they needed, as evidenced by the fact that their desire for a king ultimately led to bondage and their destruction as a nation. The reason behind their request was sinful, driven by fear and profane carnality (see 1 Samuel 8:4-9). The prophet Samuel rebuked them for desiring a king that would be just like the greedy, self-serving kings of the surrounding pagan nations (see 1 Samuel 12:12-13). The king is the supreme ruler, and the shallow spirituality of God's people resulted in failure to rest in the fact that God was their Supreme Ruler and that He would protect them. However, while it remained true that God alone was the ultimate King of Israel and over all of creation, human kings would have a key role to play in God's Kingdom.

God gave His people what they wanted by appointing Saul as the first king of Israel. The Spirit of God came on Saul, and God manifested His power through him. Saul prophesied. He was victorious in battle because God was with him. He overcame his shyness and walked with great authority. But he became inflated with all this success, and he began to rely on the arm of flesh and his own decisions. Saul was only the first in a long line of kings who yielded to the temptation to rule their way instead of God's way. The Bible says of king after king that they "did what was evil in the sight of the Lord" (2 Kings 13:2). That phrase appears fifteen times in 1 and 2 Kings to summarize the reigns of various kings. Each of them either loved power, money, conquest, or women too much, or they relied on politics instead of God. There were a few who genuinely loved God, but even they were flawed. None of them was that King God promised back in Genesis 3. None of them had a passion for spreading God's Kingdom reign, realm, or redemption from Genesis 12. There's a pattern of continually falling short. Even Solomon, the wisest of the kings, "did evil in the sight of the Lord" (1 Kings 11:6). But throughout those years of constant failure, God never forgot His promises. Those kings were only a poor approximation to God's ideal of kingship, but throughout those years of constant failure, He never forgot His promises. He began to promise through his prophets that one day He would send His own king, anointed with His Spirit, to reign in righteousness and peace over all peoples and forever.

God Promised a Final King

The best king of Israel was David, whom God called "a man after His own heart" (1 Samuel 13:14). He was a good king who loved God's word and meditated on it day and night. He even wrote most of the Psalms. Although he came nearest to the type of king God wanted, he still had flaws, and he didn't bring God's perfect reign, realm, or redemption. But his consummate desire was to build a temple for God to help bring about those things. Instead, God gave the honor of building the temple to David's son Solomon, but He gave a greater blessing to David, a promise as great as the one He gave to Abraham years earlier. A temple can be destroyed, but the gift that God gave to David will endure forever: "Your house and your kingdom shall be established forever before you. Your throne shall be established forever" (2 Samuel 7:16). That promise became the basis of Israel's future expectations and hope.

The significance of this promise goes much further than Israel. David understood that ultimately his throne would rule over all the earth and God would bless the world through the throne of David. God promised David that the future King would come through his lineage. He will restore the realm of heaven on earth. He will abolish evil, establish justice, bring peace, and conquer death. He will redeem God's broken people. He will be called God's anointed one. God anointed prophets, priests, and kings in Israel as a symbol that they served with His divine authority on them. The Hebrew word for "anointed one" is "Messiah." The Greek word for "anointed one," and thus equivalent to "Messiah," is "Christos," or Christ. This Messiah or Christ is not going to be a normal human king. He will be God Himself stepping down into our world.

One of the most significant elements found in the prophetic message is the establishment of God's Kingdom through a descendant of David, the Messiah. According to the prophets, the coming Messiah will establish God's Kingdom, transforming creation and bringing blessing to all the nations, thereby fulfilling the purpose of God's covenant with Abraham. In verse 7 of Isaiah's famous chapter 9, he speaks of the endless government of the Messiah on the throne of David. Jeremiah 23:5 describes the King as David's "Branch of righteousness," who "shall reign and prosper, and execute judgment and righteousness in the earth." The prophet makes similar pronouncements in Jeremiah 30:9 and 33:14-26. Ezekiel identifies "the one shepherd" who shall feed Israel in the last days as David (34:23-24, 37:24-25). He calls the Messiah David, because He was descended from David according to the flesh and because

He was the person in whom all the promises made to David were fulfilled.

The Bible describes clearly four characteristics of the Messiah's kingdom. First, it would be *just.* The Messiah would have righteousness as "the belt of His loins" (Isaiah 11:1-5), and He would "execute judgment and righteousness in the earth" (Jeremiah 23:5-6). The Messiah's reign would bring *peace.* In His reign, "Israel will dwell safely" (Jeremiah 23:6; Ezekiel 35:25-31). His kingdom would be *eternal,* established forever by "an everlasting covenant" (Isaiah 55:3; 2 Samuel 7:12-16). The Messiah's kingdom would be *universal.* "His dominion shall be from sea to sea, and from the river to the ends of the earth" (Zechariah 9:10). Ultimately, God's promise to Abraham in Genesis 12:3 would be fulfilled, that in his seed "all the families of the earth shall be blessed. Isaiah 9:6-7 brings together these four ideals of the kingdom. The kingdom of the Child to be born, as He sat "upon the throne of David," would be established "with judgment and justice . . . forever." His government and peace would "increase" (spread), and "there will be no end."

Unfortunately, this promise to David didn't work out so well at first. As we have seen, most of Israel's kings failed to rule over Israel in righteousness, failing to make Israel a "holy nation and kingdom of priests" and "a light to the nations." God could not accomplish His purposes for the world through Israel because of fallen and sinful kings. The whole nation fell into godlessness and evil, and finally, God allowed the Babylonians to destroy Jerusalem and take the people to be taken into captivity in 586 BC, effectively ending earthly kingship over Israel. So, what happened to the promise that David's throne would last forever? Let David himself and the prophets answer that question.

A few examples from the Psalms show that David's throne was everlasting. Psalm 18:50 declares the mercy of God to David's descendants "forevermore." Psalm 89 is a pure anthem of testimony to the promise made to David, declaring that God has sworn that David's seed and David's throne are secure forever, as surely as the sun and moon exist. Psalm 132:11 promises with another oath that the fruit of David's body will sit on David's throne forever.

Daniel declared that the Kingdom would be everlasting: "I was watching in the night visions, and behold, One like the Son of Man, coming with the clouds of heaven! He came to the Ancient of Days, and they brought Him near before Him. Then to Him was given dominion and glory and a kingdom, that all peoples, nations, and languages should serve Him. His dominion is an everlasting dominion, which shall not pass away, and His kingdom the one which shall not be destroyed" (Daniel 7:13-14; see 2:44).

The Old Testament prophets, before, during, and after the Babylonian captivity, made it clear that God would not, and did not, abandon His intention to rule over His people and His world through a Davidic king. Because of the utter sinfulness of the human heart, the prophets of Israel revealed that the only hope for the establishment of an enduring and faithful kingdom would lie in a future work of God's redemption, sovereignly accomplished through a kingly Messiah. But the heavenly messenger Gabriel, in his announcement to Mary concerning the birth of Jesus, gave the clearest witness of all to the fulfillment of God's promise to David: "He will be great, and will be called the Son of the Highest; and the Lord God will give Him the throne of His father David. And He will reign over the house of Jacob forever, and of His kingdom there will be no end" (Luke 1:32-33).

The many messianic prophecies of the Old Testament were the basis for the hopes and expectations of Israel, particularly during the turbulent years of their history between the Old and the New Testaments. Israel was oppressed by the influence and domination of one foreign power after another until the nation was brought under the complete subjugation of the Romans in 63 B.C. Like Simeon (Luke 2:25-32), God's people eagerly awaited the arrival of their deliverer and passed down this expectation to their children and grandchildren. For generations and generations, God's people looked forward to and watched for the Messiah. Unfortunately, as we shall discuss later, their idea of a Messiah developed into the notion of a warrior-king from David's line who would rule Israel. He would be a figure of grandeur and power who would overthrow the enemies of the Jews and establish the Davidic kingdom in Jerusalem.

In their desperation for an earthly king and an earthly kingdom, most of the Jews disregarded certain prophetic words about what their future Messiah and Deliverer would endure, such as those found in Psalm 22 and Isaiah 53. Consequently, as we shall see, Jesus was not what they wanted, "and His own did not receive Him" (John 1:11).

The Certainty of the Kingdom

Here is the heart of the Old Testament. It reveals God's promise of a Kingdom characterized by peace, righteousness, universality, and permanence, and prepares for its fulfillment in the coming of the Messiah. God gave the promise in Eden, and He chose a man, Abraham, to father a nation through which He would accomplish His plan. Moses, in one of the greatest speeches of history, underscored the uniqueness of that nation when he expressed his dying farewell to the descendants of Abraham. He reminded them that God had chosen them as a holy nation and warned them of the pagan lifestyles and philosophies surrounding them. Through the centuries the promise was still valid, despite the failure of Israel to exhibit the qualities of God's rule. They defied God's laws; they rejected God's prophets; and they compromised God's rule. God chose another man, David, to whom He renewed the promise of a righteous and everlasting kingdom.

UNDERSTANDING THE KINGDOM

The Theme of the Bible

We have seen that the Kingdom of God is the central theme of the Old Testament. As God established Israel as a nation and as He called them back to a relationship with Him, His concern was His Kingdom. The Kingdom is also the theme of the New Testament. The first sermon in the New Testament was from John the Baptist: "Repent, for the kingdom of heaven is at hand" (Matthew 3:2). While Jesus was on the earth, the focus of His teaching and ministry was on the Kingdom of God. The phrases "Kingdom of God," "Kingdom of heaven," and "the Kingdom" occur more than ninety times in the Gospels, and the book of Acts is filled with accounts of works of the Kingdom of God. The ministry of Jesus began with this message: "From that time Jesus began to preach and to say, 'Repent, for the kingdom of heaven is at hand'" (Matthew 4:17). His ministry ended the same way, when during the days between His resurrection and His ascension He taught His disciples "of the things pertaining to the kingdom of God" (Acts 1:3). That was His constant message all through His ministry, and because Jesus spent so much of His time teaching about the Kingdom of God, it is obviously an essential part of our understanding of the gospel. Not only can we understand God's Kingdom, but we can live in it and carry its message. Notice the following representative passages in the teachings of Jesus:

"Blessed are the poor in spirit, for theirs is the kingdom of heaven" (Matthew 5:3).

"But seek first the kingdom of God and His righteousness" (Matthew 6:33).

"But if I cast out demons by the Spirit of God, surely the kingdom of God has come upon you" (Matthew 12:28).

"It has been given to you to know the mysteries of the kingdom of heaven, but to them it has not been given" (Matthew 13:11).

"It is easier for a camel to go through the eye of a needle than for a rich man to enter the kingdom of God" (Matthew 19:24).

The Lord gave instructions concerning entrance into the kingdom of God (Matthew 21:31-43).

"Assuredly I say to you, I will no longer drink of the fruit of the vine until that day when I drink it new in the kingdom of God" (Mark 14:25).

"I must preach the kingdom of God to the other cities also, because for this purpose I have been sent" (Luke 4:43).

Jesus commissioned His disciples "to preach the kingdom of God and to heal the sick" (Luke 9:2).

When Jesus sent the 70 out, twice He instructed them to declare, "The kingdom of God has come near to you" (Luke 10:9, 11).

He proclaimed to the Pharisees, "The kingdom of God is within you" (Luke 17:21)

"Unless one is born again, he cannot see the kingdom of God" (John 3:3).

"My kingdom is not of this world" (John 18:36).

The apostle Paul emphasized the Kingdom of God in his preaching: "And he went into the synagogue and spoke boldly for three months, reasoning and persuading concerning the things of the kingdom of God" (Acts 19:8). "The kingdom of God is not eating and drinking, but righteousness and peace and joy in the Holy Spirit" (Romans 14:17). Even in prison Paul was "preaching the kingdom of God" (Acts 28:31).

The apostle Peter gave assurance that "an entrance will be supplied to you abundantly into the everlasting kingdom of our Lord and Savior Jesus Christ" (2 Peter 1:11).

James wrote, "Has God not chosen the poor of this world to be rich in faith and heirs of the kingdom which He promised to those who love Him?" (James 2:5)

The angels proclaim the eternity and triumph of the Kingdom of God: "The kingdoms of this world have become the kingdoms of our Lord and of His Christ and He shall reign forever and ever" (Revelation 11:15). "Now salvation, and strength, and the kingdom of our God, and the power of His Christ have come, or the accuser of our brethren, who accused them before our God day and night, has been cast down" (Revelation 12:10).

Material and Spiritual

So, what is the Kingdom of God? That's a good question, and it's profoundly important that we grasp its meaning. The Bible shows us that God is sovereign over two domains, the material kingdom and the spiritual kingdom. When God created out of His sovereign will and by His spoken word, He made things material, and He made persons spiritual. And He is King over both domains. This is the universal, eternal sovereignty of God over everything He has made, everything animate and inanimate, everything material, everything spiritual in the universe. It's essential that we keep in mind these two areas in which God exercises His sovereign rule if we are to understand His unfolding purpose in the world. First, there is the external universal kingdom over which He rules by creation. We have already presented the biblical teaching that God is forever the King of everything that He has created. "The Lord is King forever and ever" (Psalm 10:16). "The Lord sits as King forever" (Psalm 29:10). "The Lord has established His throne in heaven, and His kingdom rules over all" (Psalm 103:19). "They shall speak of the glory of Your kingdom and talk of Your power, to make known to the sons of men His mighty acts, and the glorious majesty of His kingdom. Your kingdom is an everlasting kingdom, and Your dominion endures throughout all generations" (Psalm 145:11-13).

So, God is King over the external, universal kingdom, which includes everything He has created. He is also King over the internal, personal kingdom, which includes everyone He has recreated. He rules one by creation. He rules another by recreation, through a new birth. It is through the transformed hearts of men and women that this Kingdom comes and is on the earth. Jesus said of this Kingdom that it is "not of this world" (John 18:36). This is the Kingdom with which we are concerned. Later in this chapter, we will consider more fully the biblical teachings about the spiritual kingdom, but first, we must examine some erroneous views of the Kingdom of God.

False Views of the Kingdom

The Kingdom of God touches every part of life, and if we are wrong in understanding it, or if we distort its teaching, then we will get everything else wrong, not only the gospel itself, but politics, education, ethics, race, social relationships, and so it goes. The people who heard Jesus teach had formed their own image of what the Kingdom of God was supposed to be, and many others since then have done likewise. There are several common misinterpretations of the kingdom of God.

Nationalism

The Jews of the first century studied the Scriptures diligently, and they knew what the Old Testament promised. They saw that everything contained in the Old Testament was, in one way or another, about God's Kingdom. To them, the dominant theme of the Old Testament description of the future Messiah is a conquering king, who will vanquish all of Israel's enemies and reestablish the glorious Davidic kingdom, with Jerusalem as its capital. The promises of the Kingdom touched every aspect of human life. It was a political hope, that there would be no injustice and no oppression. There will be prevailing peace and joy and comfort. Evil governments will be destroyed, and a king like David, even greater than David, will be on the throne. The Messiah will be a powerful political ruler, and there will be nobles around Him ruling as vice-regents with Him in the glory of restored Israel. All nations will be subjected to Him and He will reign in triumph. Israel will be the crowning nation of the world, and the jewel in the crown will be the city of Jerusalem, which will rise to prominence over all cities. This is what the people expected because the prophets had spelled it out. In the first century, the Romans were the overlords, and common to every Jewish scenario of the coming of the Kingdom was the Messiah's expulsion of these hated Gentiles who ruled over them. Near the time that the Romans invaded Israel, a Jewish writer, posing as Solomon, wrote a psalm that bears passionate witness to Jewish hopes for the coming Kingdom:

> See, Lord, and raise up for them their king,
> the son of David, to rule over your servant Israel
> in the time known to you, O God.
> Undergird him with the strength to destroy the unrighteous rulers,
> to purge Jerusalem from gentiles . . .
> He will gather a holy people
> whom he will lead in righteousness . . . .
> And he will be a righteous king over them, taught by God.
> There will be no unrighteousness among them in his days,
> for all shall be holy,
> and their king shall be the Lord Messiah. (*Psalms of Solomon* 17)

Thus, when Jesus proclaimed the arrival of the Kingdom, He was speaking to people who fervently hoped and prayed for its coming. Yet He did not fulfill their common expectations concerning how the Kingdom would come. He didn't raise up an army to lead a rebellion against Rome, and He didn't promise the establishment of a political kingdom.

The Jewish concept of the Kingdom involved economic hope. In this glorious Kingdom, there will be no poverty, hunger, famine, or deprivation. There will be the absence of sickness, and people will enjoy long life. It was even an environmental hope. The curse on the earth will be reversed. The whole topography of the planet will be changed, and the Lord will create a river flowing from Jerusalem out to make the desert blossom like a rose.

Above all, their Messianic hope was a spiritual hope. The whole nation will be blessed, the whole nation will become righteous and obedient, and the whole nation will know God. The power of sin will be destroyed, and God's people will enjoy an intimacy with Him beyond anything that was ever known in the past. Furthermore, Yahweh will be universally worshiped around the world as the one true God.

Essentially, the people were looking forward to all these idealistic characteristics, but there were a lot of misconceptions in their view of the Kingdom of God. Their error stemmed from the fact that they did not expect that the Messiah would come to establish an internal spiritual Kingdom. Simply put, that's why they rejected Jesus and why His message was so offensive to them. They weren't looking for a Savior because they didn't need to be saved. It wasn't that they weren't looking for a King or didn't want the Kingdom. It was the kind of Kingdom Jesus was talking about that upset them.

Sad to say, but even the apostles, who had shared the traditional views of the Kingdom, were slow to understand the teachings of Jesus about the Kingdom of God. When they started to follow Jesus, they had a different leader in mind. They had the idea that Jesus would one day overthrow the Roman yoke of bondage. That's why the sons of Zebedee asked for special seats in the kingdom. They were anticipating a worldly kingdom, and they wanted to share in that power and authority. The disciples were not expecting Jesus to die on the cross. A study of the Gospels shows that every time Jesus brought up the cross, they tried to change the subject. They had not chosen to follow a Christ who was going to be humble and humiliated and act as a servant and finally die on a Roman cross.

Even after the resurrection, the apostles asked Jesus, "Lord, will You at this time restore the kingdom to Israel?" (Acts 1:6). I have often wondered how that question affected the risen Lord. The Kingdom of God was the essence of His instruction to them. After one intensive session of teaching, He asked them, "Have you understood all these things?" Without hesitation they responded, "Yes, Lord" (Matthew 13:51). But the question of Acts 1:6 reveals that even after all the teaching Jesus had shared with them, they were still slow to comprehend the full meaning of the Kingdom. We learn several truths from the patient response of Jesus.

First, the Kingdom of God is spiritual in its character. It cannot be located on any map of the world, because it's the rule of God in the lives of people. The question of the apostles showed that they were still dreaming of a territorial kingdom in which Israel would be liberated from the yoke of Rome. Instead of giving a direct answer to their question, Jesus spoke about the Holy Spirit coming upon them and empowering them to bear witness to Him. His statements make it clear that the Kingdom of God was the reign of God in the hearts and lives of people. His Kingdom would be spread by witnesses, not by armies; through a gospel of peace, not a declaration of war; by the power of the Holy Spirit, not by force of arms or political dominion.

The response of Jesus also shows us that the Kingdom of God is international in its membership. The apostles asked about the restoration of the Kingdom to Israel, revealing their narrow nationalism. The Jews rightly believed that they were God's chosen people, but they missed the point of the purpose for which God chose them. God chose them for responsibility, not privilege, but for centuries they had been taught that God loved only Israel of all the nations He created. The Jews fiercely despised Gentiles, and some rabbis taught that the only reason that God created Gentiles was so they would be fuel for the fires of hell. But in verse 8 of His reply to the apostles, Jesus told them that the Holy Spirit would give them the power to witness not only "in Jerusalem and in all Judea," but far beyond the borders of Israel. After Judea, they would take the gospel to the hated region of Samaria, and then to Gentile nations throughout the earth. A reading of the book of Acts shows that the first Christian witnesses followed in order the outline given in Acts 1:8.

The missionary commission that Jesus gave shows that the Kingdom of God knows nothing of exclusive, restrictive nationalism. Contrary to first-century Jewish expectations, it is an international Kingdom in which there are no natural barriers of race, culture, nation, or tribe. The Bible tells us that when the Kingdom is consummated in heaven, it will include "a great multitude which no one could number, of all nations, tribes, peoples, and tongues" (Revelation 7:9).

Jesus also showed that the Kingdom of God is gradual in its expansion. The apostles asked if the restoration of the Kingdom to Israel would be "at this time." Evidently, they had expected it to happen during His ministry, but that hope had been destroyed by His crucifixion. Now that He was resurrected, would He do what they had hoped He would do earlier, and would He do it immediately? In response, Jesus first cautioned against fruitless and unfounded curiosity and speculation about dates: "It is not for you to know times or seasons which the Father has put in His own authority" (Acts 1:7). Then He spoke to them about being His witnesses in gradually widening circles between the Spirit's coming upon them and His own coming again (verse 8). In fact, the entire interval between the Lord's ascension and His return was to be marked by missionary activity. The charge was to witness to the end of the earth (verse 8) and to the end of the age (Matthew 28:20). Those two ends will coincide because Jesus said that only when the gospel had been preached to all nations would the end come (Matthew 24:14).

It's not difficult to understand why the Jews rejected Jesus, because He did not fulfill their concept of the Messiah as a great warrior who would establish the Kingdom through military conquest.

Sectarianism

Those with a sectarian view of the Kingdom of God equate it with a narrow, exclusive group. For example, during the time of the ministry of Jesus on earth, it was the Pharisees who thought they had a monopoly on the Kingdom of God because of their system of rigid legalism and religious traditions. Everybody else was excluded. Of course, Jesus exposed the fallacy of this view when He pointed to the faith of the Roman centurion in Matthew 8:11-12: "And I say to you that many will come from east and west, and sit down with Abraham, Isaac, and Jacob in the kingdom of heaven. But the sons of the kingdom will be cast out into outer darkness. There will be weeping and gnashing of teeth." The implication of this saying is abundantly clear: no matter where it comes from, faith in Jesus assures a place in the Kingdom.

There are those who think that their affiliation with a certain denominational group guarantees their access to the Kingdom of God. In other words, some equate the Kingdom of God with a particular denomination. Hence, there is a fragmentation among Christians in which some groups meet in their own exclusive corner of God's universe, maintaining the belief that nobody else matters outside of themselves. Their gospel is, "Come and join us; we've got all the truth here!" In effect, they reduce Jesus and the Kingdom to the size of their own group.

Such a sectarian mentality ignores the personal dimension of the Kingdom, centering on Jesus, its head. Like Nicodemus, people with this kind of sectarian persuasion are slow to grasp that being in the Kingdom means being born again spiritually from above, by the inward working of the Holy Spirit. As we shall see later, the church is definitely closely involved in the Kingdom of God, but the actual scope of the Kingdom is far wider than the church. It ultimately extends to the entirety of the created order, when all things will be under the feet of Jesus Christ (1 Corinthians 15:27).

Humanism

In relation to the Kingdom of God, this view is a product of secular humanism, with its social, human-based outlook. Religious humanism thinks of the Kingdom of God in materialistic, socio-political, economic, and environmental terms. Adherents of this view interpret the gospel in the context of a human utopia in which all the material and social needs of all mankind are met. Closely akin to this perspective is so-called liberation theology, which emphasizes liberation from social, political, and economic oppression as an anticipation of ultimate salvation. Other groups, such as black liberation theology and feminist liberation theology, fit into this category.

If you misuse the Bible, you can make it mean anything, and in this case, the Kingdom of God is interpreted as a political revolution that provides a panacea for all the oppression caused by an unjust society. All Christians should share the indignation of humanists at the terrible poverty and gross inequities of society, and the Bible condemns injustice and oppression. Jesus Himself described His mission as a mission of liberation, and His words and compassionate deeds give evidence that He wasn't just referring to a mystical type of spiritual liberation. He announced in Luke 4:18-19: "The Spirit of the Lord is upon Me, because He has anointed Me to preach the gospel to the poor; He has sent Me to heal the brokenhearted, to proclaim liberty to the captives and recovery of sight to the blind, to set at liberty those who are oppressed; to proclaim the acceptable year of the Lord."

Liberation from oppression is a good thing, and it is a major topic in biblical teaching and a vital characteristic of the Kingdom of God. Yet, to make it *the* defining centerpiece of Kingdom theology takes a lot more than tracing the theme through a few Scriptures. The glaring error of this view is that it ignores the spiritual nature of the Kingdom of God and Christ's kingly rule (see John 18:36). As important as feeding the hungry is, it cannot take the place of the gospel of Christ (see Acts 3:6). The so-called social gospel fails to recognize that the basic problem in the world is sin, the consequences of which are evident in every area of life. Those consequences, which include oppression and inequity, are outward symptoms of a spiritual problem. When the Bible addresses those external problems, it does so in full recognition of the underlying root cause of sin. The world's *primary* need is spiritual, not social. But the liberationists, influenced more by Marxism than the Bible, fail to recognize this reality and thus fail to recognize the best way to aid those trapped in poverty and oppression, leaving only revolution and violence as the means of solving the problem. Liberationists must also recognize that the gospel is for all people, including the rich (Luke 2:10). To assign special status to any group as being preferred by God is to discriminate, something God does not do (Acts 10:34-35). Christ brings unity to His church, not division along socio-economic, racial, or gender lines (Galatians 3:28).

Dualism

In a theological context pertaining to supreme power, dualism asserts that there are two parallel and eternal opposing kingdoms of equal power. The one, headed by God is good, and the other, ruled by

Satan, is evil. The Bible does teach that there are two kingdoms, with the contrasting characteristics of good and evil, light and darkness, freedom and bondage, life and death, faith and fear, truth and deceit, hope and despair, understanding and confusion, etc. However, the struggle between good and evil, and between God and Satan, is not eternal, because only God has eternal existence. Everything else has been created by Him. Even Satan was created by God as an angel before he rebelled (see Isaiah 14:12-15; Ezekiel 28:13-17). As a created being, the devil has none of the divine attributes that God possesses. The devil is not all-powerful, all-knowing, or everywhere present. He is not God's opposite. Furthermore, evil does not have eternal existence. Everything was perfect, with no evil anywhere, when God finished creating the heavens and the universe (see Genesis 1:31). Evil only entered the earth with the rebellion in Eden. In addition, even though Satan has power, his power is no match to that of God. The Bible teaches that there is only one power that is omnipotent, overriding all others, and that power is God. Although Satan has not stopped trying, he never was, and never will be equal to God (see 1 John 4:4). Ultimately, Satan will be banished forever (Revelation 20:10).

Triumphalism

Many believers become so enthused and anticipative about the fulfillment of Kingdom promises that they look for the future dimensions of the Kingdom in the present, forgetting the sacrificial nature of the Kingdom. What I mean is that many people focus on the physical and economic aspects of the Kingdom to the extent that they believe that citizenship in the Kingdom of God confers immediate immunity against sickness, poverty, and all other problems. The idea is that truly knowing God and having the indwelling of the Holy Spirit puts an end to various kinds of difficulties common to mere mortals. From now on, it's "all honey, no bees; no work, all ease." Such an attitude disregards the teachings of Jesus concerning the difficulties that we will inevitably face on earth. When the disciples James and John blatantly requested that Jesus grant them places of prominence in the Kingdom, He responded to them about the cup of suffering that He would be required to accept, and that they must share as well (Mark 10:37-39). There will be persecution (see such scriptures as Matthew 5:10-12; 10:16-18; John 15:20; Galatians 4:29; 1 Thessalonians 3:3-4; 2 Timothy 3:11-12; 1 Peter 4:12-14; Revelation 2:10-11). Believers, even Christian leaders, are not lifted above the reach of sickness (see 2 Corinthians 12:9-10; Philippians 2:26-27; 1 Timothy 5:23; 2 Timothy 4:20; James 5:14; Revelation 21:4). Kingdom citizenship is not a pleasant excursion in a balloon fueled by uninterrupted glorious experiences. As we shall see later, the Kingdom of God will not reach complete fulfillment, including the destruction of sickness, sin, and death until "the end," when Christ returns in universal power and glory and "delivers the kingdom to God the Father" (1 Corinthians 15:24).

The Bible teaches that adversity is a trademark of the Kingdom of God. Jesus, having just announced His betrayal and instituting the Lord's Supper, told His apostles, "You are those who have continued with Me in My trials. And I bestow upon you a kingdom . . .." (Luke 22:28-29). That Kingdom was certainly not a trouble-free life. The apostle Paul recognized that fact, and he openly announced it: "We must through many tribulations enter the kingdom of God" (Acts 14:22). We should not deliberately seek trials, but we will inevitably face them, especially opposition.

The word translated "tribulation" (*thilipsis*) is used 45 times in the New Testament. Twenty-one times it's translated as "tribulation," and 19 times "affliction." The word carries the idea of pressure, anguish, trouble, distress, and opposition. It's a strong term that refers not to minor inconveniences but to real hardships. The word is used in James 1:27 of "orphans and widows in their trouble." It's used in 2 Corinthians 8:13 for material shortage. Jesus used the word in Matthew 7:14 in describing how "difficult" is the way that leads to life. He used the same word in Matthew 24:9 and John 16:33 when He warned that we will face "tribulation." In 1 Peter 1:6, it's used for the "trials" of persecution.

Enduring hardship, particularly as a direct result of following Jesus Christ, is a badge of Kingdom citizenship. Jesus repeatedly warned of the trials that His followers would face, such as in John 15:18-20, when He told them that they would experience the world's hatred and persecution simply because they followed Him. Speaking of the trials that they would face, He said, "When you see these things happening, know that the kingdom of God is near" (Luke 21:31). Our natural reaction to trouble is to ask, "Why is this happening to me?" as though it's something abnormal to the Christian life. But the Bible admonishes, "Do not think it strange concerning the fiery trial which is to try you, as though some strange thing happened to you; but rejoice to the extent that you partake of Christ's sufferings, that when His glory is revealed, you may also be glad with exceeding joy" (1 Peter 4:12-13). We are to "count it all joy" when we experience various adversities, because of the spiritual growth they bring (James 1:2).

The topic of how God uses trials as a gateway to greater kingdom citizenship is a subject for another study. Still, the point I'm making is that you are not ready to live under the rule of Jesus Christ until and unless you are ready to suffer with His sufferings. The Bible never promises life in the Kingdom without a struggle. Entering the Kingdom of God is a costly decision, and we must count the cost as Moses did. He "refused to be called the son of Pharaoh's daughter, choosing rather to suffer affliction with the people of God than to enjoy the passing pleasures of sin, esteeming the reproach of Christ greater riches than the treasures in

Egypt, for he looked to the reward" (Hebrews 11:24-26).

The presence and strength of Jesus with us through our adversities is also the subject of another study. Suffice it to say that the Bible strongly assures us that He never leaves us. Some people are fond of saying, "Jesus is a bridge over troubled waters." No, He isn't a bridge *over* troubled waters, but He is certainly the pathway *through* them. Triumph and victory may characterize the experience of each citizen of the Kingdom of God, but victory only comes through battle, and triumph only follows trial. It's an inadequate view of the truth of the Kingdom of God to teach otherwise. However, it's just as inadequate to maintain the negative view that we are predestined to experience problems and therefore we should merely tolerate them. The Bible does teach that we will experience suffering, trials, and all kinds of human difficulty, but it also teaches that all adversities may be overcome. The presence of the King and the power of His Kingdom in our lives do not make us invulnerable or immune to life's struggles, but they do bring the promise of victory, with provision for every need and strength for every weakness.

The Kingdom Explained

Having written all these things about the Kingdom of God, we still have not stated a clear, precise definition of the Kingdom. For that matter, other than illustrations of the Kingdom in the parables of Jesus and the descriptive statement in Romans 14:17, there is no single definition of the Kingdom in the Bible. As you study the Bible, you will become aware of the fact that most of the teaching about the Kingdom of God is found in the four Gospels, in the teaching of Jesus. When you get into the epistles, you will find far fewer references to the Kingdom, and yet it's the epistles that provide the basic vital exposition of Christian doctrine. Does the less frequent mention of the term "Kingdom of God" suggest that the apostles diluted the teaching of Jesus or gave less emphasis to it? Not at all, but rather the opposite. They understood that the Kingdom of God was inseparable from the person of Christ the King. The understanding that the Kingdom centers in Him was beginning to emerge during His ministry. Jesus gave concrete substance and significance to what the Kingdom is, in His person, in His teachings, and in His deeds. Peter, James, and John had a glimpse of the Kingdom and its glory when they witnessed the transfiguration of Jesus (Luke 9:28-36). At the cross, the true redemptive nature of the Kingdom and the mission of the King were clearly revealed. The resurrection vindicated the King's mission. The ascension celebrated it. The powerful outpouring of the Holy Spirit at Pentecost broadened its impact from Judea to a worldwide dimension.

In English usage, the word "kingdom" means territory over which a king rules, a realm having geographical boundaries and borders. But it's essential that we understand what Jesus meant when He spoke of the Kingdom. In the New Testament, the Greek word for kingdom (*basileia*) could sometimes refer to a place where a monarch reigned, but that isn't its primary meaning. In the first century, the predominant meaning of the word was not the land over which a king ruled, but the "rule," "authority," and "sovereignty" of the king. The same was true of the Aramaic word (*malku*), the term that Jesus likely used. Therefore, when Jesus spoke about the Kingdom of God, He was referring to *authority*, not *locality*. This meaning is quite clear in Luke 19:12, in a parable that Jesus told: "A certain nobleman went into a far country to receive for himself a kingdom (*basileia*) and to return." He did not go there to get a new territory over which to reign but to get increased authority over the place he already ruled.

The same meaning of kingdom is found in the Hebrew Old

Testament and its Greek translation, the Septuagint. Most of the psalms make use of parallelism, a common literary feature of Hebrew poetry in which something is stated twice. Something would be written and then repeated in a way that developed it or interpreted it or stated in another way. For example, in Psalm 46:1 the first part is, "God is our refuge and strength," and the second part is "A very present help in trouble." A second example is in verse 7 of the same psalm: the first part is, "The Lord of hosts is with us," and the second part is, "The God of Jacob is our refuge." Psalm 145:10-11 contains parallel statements regarding the Kingdom:

> All Your works shall praise You, O Lord,
> And Your saints shall bless you.
> They shall speak of the glory of Your kingdom (Hebrew *malkuth*; Greek *basileia*),
> And talk of Your power.

The parallel is that of God's Kingdom to His divine power, not to the territory over which He reigns. The works of God and the people of God offer praise to His sovereignty, not to the place over which He is sovereign.

Therefore, when Jesus announced in Mark 1:15, "The Kingdom of God is at hand," He didn't mean that a place where God rules had come near. He meant the arrival of God's kingly authority and sovereignty. The Kingdom of God really means the reign of God; it means the law and the rule of God; it means unquestioned obedience to His will. Jesus taught us to pray, "Your kingdom come. Your will be done on earth as it is in heaven" (Matthew 6:10). This two-fold petition is another example of Hebrew parallelism, in which the will of God interprets the Kingdom of God. The two are inseparably linked. When we pray, "Your Kingdom come," we are praying on a personal level that we might obey God's will the way the angels obey it in heaven (see Psalm 103:21). We are praying for heavenly obedience, the same fervency and undivided submission that the angels have. But this prayer is on the worldwide level, that the gospel will spread around the world and that every knee on earth might bend in submission to the rule of God. In heaven there is total obedience to the will of God. So, when we pray, "Your will be done on earth as it is in heaven," we are praying that people on earth will do the will of God the way the angels do in heaven. In other words, we are praying for the Kingdom to come. Basically, then, the Kingdom of God is God's kingly rule—His reign, His works, His lordship, His sovereign governance— over the hearts and lives of those who willingly submit to His authority, when God's will is done on earth as perfectly as it is in heaven.

The Kingdom Located

This section deals more with where the Kingdom of God is not located than with where it is located. We have already emphasized the fact that the Kingdom of God is a reign, not a realm, that is, it is not a territory that can be located on a map. However, there are several common misunderstandings that need clarification.

The Kingdom Is Not Heaven

God does reign in heaven, but it's clear that in His proclamation of the Kingdom, Jesus was not telling us about God's rule in the afterlife. As we have seen, Jesus taught us to pray, "Your kingdom come. Your will be done on earth as it is in heaven." Notice that we are to pray for the Kingdom to come, indicating that it is not a place to which we go after death. Furthermore, as we have also seen, the use of Hebrew parallelism equates the Kingdom with the will of God. Currently, God reigns in heaven and therefore His will is done, but we are to pray for God's Kingdom to come, and for his will to be done *on earth*. Much of the confusion comes from the fact that the Gospel of Matthew uses the term "Kingdom of heaven" 32 times, whereas the other Gospels use the term "the Kingdom of God." Why the difference? Matthew wrote for a primarily Jewish audience who were familiar with the Scriptures. They already understood the concept of the Kingdom of God based on their knowledge of the writings of the prophets. For example, Daniel 2:44 speaks of "the God of heaven [who] will set up a kingdom which will never be destroyed," and "His kingdom is an everlasting kingdom" (Daniel 4:3). In speaking of this Kingdom, Jewish teachers would use the Hebrew phrase *makur shamayim,* meaning "kingdom of heaven." Jews revered the holy name of God, Yahweh, and they would not speak the name directly. They would often substitute the word "heaven" when referring to God. The term "Kingdom of heaven" is less direct than "Kingdom of God" and is therefore more agreeable to Jewish sensibilities. We do essentially the same when we use such expressions as "heaven forbid," or "heaven was good to me today."

There is no significant difference between the Kingdom of God and the Kingdom of heaven. Jesus made no distinction between the two in His conversation with the rich young ruler, but used them interchangeably, apparently considering them synonymous (Matthew 19:23-24). Moreover, in frequent parallel accounts of the same parable, Mark and Luke used "kingdom of God" whereas Matthew used "kingdom of heaven." Compare Matthew 11:11-12 with Luke 7:18; Matthew 13:11 with Mark 4:11 and Luke 8:10; Matthew 13:24 with Mark 4:26; Matthew 13:31 with Mark 4:30 and Luke 13:18; Matthew 13:33 with Luke 13:20; Matthew 18:3 with Mark 10:14 and Luke 18:16; and Matthew 22:2 with Luke 13:29. Clearly, the two phrases refer to the same thing.

The phrase "Kingdom of God" emphasizes the sovereign Ruler of the kingdom, while the phrase "Kingdom of heaven" indicates the source from which the power and authority of the Kingdom come, but they are the same Kingdom. The Kingdom ruled by Christ will come to earth from heaven with the power and the authority of God.

The Kingdom Is Not the Church

The relationship between the Church and the Kingdom has often been the subject of debate. The Kingdom of God is not the Church, yet there is an inseparable relationship between the two, and the Church is essential to the fulfillment of the Kingdom. Let's understand that the capitalized word "Church" refers to the universal body of believers, while the word in lower case refers to a building or to a local gathering of believers. Think of the Church as the meeting of the citizens of the Kingdom, those who know the rule of God. The word translates the Greek word *ekklesia*, which literally means "called out ones." As we have seen, the Kingdom of God refers primarily to the sovereign rule and reign of God. When Jesus said that He would build His Church (Matthew 16:18), He was referring to a community of believers through whom the righteous reign of God would be demonstrated. It lives by new values and standards, and its relationships have been transformed by love. The Church is the body of which Christ is the head (Ephesians 1:22-23; Colossians 1:18).

The church is part of the Kingdom of God, but not all of it. The Church is essential to the fulfillment of the Kingdom. The Kingdom comes as a result of the preaching of the gospel of the Kingdom in the world. That preaching of the gospel, is, through the apostles, entrusted to the Church (Matthew 28:19; Acts 1:8). The central place of the Church in God's Kingdom is also highlighted by the fact that in the apostles the keys of the Kingdom have been given to the Church (Matthew 16:19). The function of the Church, among other things, is to nurture the new life of Kingdom citizens through teaching, worship, and fellowship to bring them into spiritual maturity, "to the measure of the stature of the fulness of Christ" (Ephesians 4:13). The Church also provides weapons for spiritual warfare against the kingdom of darkness. The Kingdom of God existed before the beginning of the Church, and it will continue after the mission of the Church to proclaim the Kingdom is complete. Meanwhile, in the present age, the Kingdom of God expresses itself most visibly through the Church. The Church is the first fruits of the redeemed humanity (James 1:18).

The Kingdom Is Not Merely in Our Hearts

What I mean by this heading is that the Kingdom of God is not limited to an internal subjective experience. A verse often quoted, especially by transcendentalists, to support the location of the Kingdom in the heart is Luke 17:21, where Jesus is quoted as saying, "The kingdom of God is within you." However, to get the full meaning of this statement, we need to consider the context in which it was spoken. It's important that we understand that Jesus was not talking to His faithful followers. He was responding to a question that a group of hostile Pharisees had just asked Him. They asked when the Kingdom of God was coming. That question was a challenge to the authenticity of Jesus, because the Pharisees thought of the Kingdom of God as a literal physical kingdom, appearing with all kinds of spectacular signs, most notably a successful revolt against the tyranny of Rome, led by the Messiah. But in His reply, Jesus pointedly told them that their expectations were misguided. He said, "The kingdom of God does not come with observation; nor will they say, 'See here!' or 'See there!' For indeed, the kingdom of God is within you" (Luke 17:20-21).

Considering that Jesus described the hearts of the Pharisees as "full of extortion and self-indulgence" and "all uncleanness" (Matthew 23:25, 27), it's highly unlikely that on this occasion He is telling them to look into their own sinful hearts if they want to find the Kingdom. The key to understanding the statement of Jesus in Luke 17:21 is the translation of the Greek word *entos*. Some versions, including the King James Version, the New King James Version, and the American Standard Version, translate the word as "within." However, if you have such a version and it has center-column references or footnotes, you will probably see that an alternate translation is "among" or "in the midst of." Almost all the modern versions use either "among" or "in the midst of" in translating the Greek word. So, Jesus was saying to the Pharisees, "If you want to find the Kingdom, look around you. It's already here, right before your eyes. See My works and see citizens of the Kingdom standing around you." All the power, glory, majesty, authority, and rulership of God's Kingdom was right there, right among them, drawn so very near to them, in the person of Jesus Christ.

It's true that the Kingdom of God lies within the heart by virtue of the Spirit of God dwelling inside the believer and transforming life, but it is not limited to an internal experience. The Kingdom of God impacts all aspects of earthly life—in family, community, cultural, racial, political, economic, gender, generational, and institutional relationships. It affects individual believers but also touches the world around them. We emphasize again that the Kingdom of God is where God's will and desire are being done; a place where God is in control. When Kingdom citizens live their lives in complete submission to God's control and with the power of the Holy Spirit, they become a positive, godly influence on society, like the permeating qualities of salt and light. They exhibit the Kingdom of God in action because they demonstrate the characteristics of Jesus Christ as the Holy Spirit transforms them into the likeness of Jesus and produces His fruit in them.

The Kingdom Is Not of This World

Does this heading sound contradictory to the thought of the Kingdom of God on earth? There is no contradiction because the words "earth" and "world" carry two completely different connotations. When we speak of the earth, we mean a literal physical place, the planet on which we live. While the Bible many times uses the word "world" to mean the physical earth and/or the people who inhabit the earth, it often uses it in a moral or spiritual sense to denote an ungodly value system, an environment hostile to the rule of God, and the hostile people who reject God and His ways. In the broadest sense, the term "world" sums up evil and corruption. Satan rules this world (John 12:31; 14:30; 16:11; 2 Corinthians 4:4), and it is full of corruption (2 Peter 1:4). It's impossible to be friendly with the evil world and love God at the same time (James 4:4; 1 John 2:15-17). By their faith Kingdom citizens must "overcome the world" (1 John 5:4-5), killing whatever belongs to their earthly nature (Colossians 3:5) and denying "worldly lusts" (Titus 2:12). The world hates Jesus (John 7:7) and will hate His followers (John 15:18-19). The world, that is, ungodly people, cannot receive the things of God (John 14:17, 22; 16:8-9; 1 John 3:1) and is not even worthy of the people of faith who live among them (Hebrews 11:38).

Because of the hatred of the world, Jesus asks the Father to protect His followers while leaving them as witnesses in alien surroundings (John 17:14-17). The present world is passing away even now (1 John

2:17), but while we live in it, we must not love it (2 Timothy 4:10) or become conformed to its ways (Romans 12:2). We must beware of its godless "wisdom" (1 Corinthians 2:6; 3:18-19; James 3:15). Positively, we must live a godly life (Titus 2:12), realizing that by His death Jesus has delivered us from "this present evil age" (Galatians 1:4). At the same time, we "look for new heavens and a new earth in which righteousness dwells" (2 Peter 3:13).

Jesus plainly declared that His Kingdom "is not of this world" (John 18:36). He spoke those words to Pilate after the Jewish priests had brought Him to the Roman governor for official judgment. The Romans had taken from them the power of capital punishment, so in their hatred of Jesus, they trumped up a false accusation against Him that Pilate could not ignore, even though he was skeptical. The charge was that Jesus claimed to be a king, and if the charge were true, then He was a threat to the empire. Pilate asked Jesus pointedly, "Are you a king then?" (John 18:37). In our vernacular the answer that Jesus gave would be something like, "Correct, you said it!"

During Pilate's interrogation, Jesus spoke a very definitive statement about the Kingdom that must be closely considered in any study of the Kingdom of God. He said: "My kingdom is not of this world. If My kingdom were of this world, My servants would fight, so that I should not be delivered to the Jews; but now My kingdom is not from here" (verse 36). Literally, His Kingdom is not out of this world. It is not laid alongside this world for comparison. It is not like this world. The Greek word translated "from here" (*enteuthen*) literally means "from the same as," or "on both sides." If His Kingdom had been of the world, His followers would have fought to save Him, that is, they would have used worldly methods to obtain their goal.

Throughout history, the Church has always faced the temptation to make the Kingdom of God a Kingdom of the world. We have already seen the expectations of the Jews and the slow understanding of the apostles concerning the Kingdom. Constantine, the emperor of Rome AD306-337, did unspeakable harm to the Church when he declared it the state religion, making it a kingdom of the world. Jesus refused to use worldly methods to build the Kingdom, but many professing Christians are following the wrong Jesus and have yielded to the temptation to use the methods of the world. Hence, the compromise with the world, the use of gimmicks, and a distorted gospel to attract people. The values of this world have no value in the true Kingdom of God.

The Kingdom Described

Parables

During His ministry, Jesus told a series of descriptive stories, each presenting a facet of the Kingdom, several of which are found in Matthew 13. The Kingdom is like seeds being sown on different kinds of soil, depicting different reactions to the preaching of the Kingdom. The Kingdom grows side by side with evil, like good wheat among weeds, with a separation at the end. Like a tiny mustard seed that grows into a huge tree, the Kingdom has a small beginning, but it's destined for greatness, with citizens from all parts, because it's a universal Kingdom. The Kingdom grows slowly, mysteriously, and unspectacularly, like yeast steadily working its way through the dough. The Kingdom is like a treasure hidden in a field that gives true joy and fulfillment when it's discovered and obtained. The Kingdom is more valuable than anything else, as illustrated by a pearl salesman who is willing to sacrifice and surrender all that he has in order to obtain one pearl of great value. The Kingdom will culminate in the eternal separation of the good from the evil, the true from the false, like a net that gathered a great catch of various kinds of fish that were sorted between the keepers and the rejects. Instruction concerning the Kingdom is like a householder who brings both old and new things out of his treasure. The old refers to knowledge of the Kingdom long possessed from the teachings of the Old Testament. The new refers to new revelations of God's truth through Jesus.

Righteousness, Peace, Joy

Romans 14:17 tells us that "the kingdom of God is not eating and drinking, but righteousness and peace and joy in the Holy Spirit." This statement is more descriptive than definitive, meaning that Paul is writing about certain characteristics of the Kingdom. This verse is part of a larger context in which the apostle warns believers against judging one another according to their views concerning outward rules and regulations. There was friction in the Church between Jewish and Gentile believers concerning what was acceptable in eating and drinking and which days should be considered holy. The gist of Paul's teaching in response to the situation is that the Kingdom of God involves more than outward ritual performance. It's a matter of obeying the leading of the Holy Spirit, not following a rigid set of rules and regulations.

Underlying the statement of Romans 14:17 is the truth that it's not the subjects who set the standards of the Kingdom; it's the King who sets the standards of the Kingdom. The New Testament speaks of righteousness in a two-fold sense. First, there is *imputed* righteousness, given to us through faith in Jesus Christ, and declaring our right standing before God. When we received Jesus Christ as our Lord and Savior, the Holy Spirit entered our lives and gave us spiritual life. God the Father now sees us as justified, not because of our own merit, but through the sacrifice of Jesus (see 2 Corinthians 5:21; Philippians 3:8-10).

There is also *actual* or *practical* righteousness, in which the believer, "having died to sins, might live for righteousness" (1 Peter 2:24). We strive to live holy lives, to be like Jesus. Once we have been imputed righteousness through faith in Jesus, we are to pursue actual righteousness (Romans 6:1-2; 11-14; 1 John 1:7; Matthew 6:33; 1 Timothy 6:11; 2 Timothy 2:22; see Proverbs 11:19, 15:9; 21:21). The righteousness in Romans 14:17 likely refers to this kind of practical righteousness as we live it out in relationships with one another. But it's also true that the practical righteousness with which we relate to each other is built on the perfect righteousness that God imputes to us by faith alone.

Next comes peace, which can mean the peace that we have with God (Romans 5:1) or the peace we have with each other (2 Corinthians 11:13). The context of Romans 14:17 indicates the peace that we enjoy with each other comes as, instead of creating an atmosphere of contention and strife by criticizing one another over non-essential issues, we "pursue the things which make for peace and the things by which one may edify another" (v. 19). Then there is joy, both a personal joy and a common joy that arises out of the peaceful and harmonious atmosphere that prevails in the church. Peace and joy are not self-produced, but Spirit-produced, for "the fruit of the Spirit is love, joy, peace . . ." (Galatians 5:22). The sequence of righteousness, peace, and joy in Romans 14:17 is parallel to that found in Romans 5:1-2, which speaks of *righteousness* imputed through faith, *peace* with God, and *joy* in the hope of His glory.

The Holy Spirit

The phrase, "in the Holy Spirit," in Romans 14:17 connects the work of the Holy Spirit with the advancement of the kingdom of God. God exercises His ruling, reigning, and dominion through the indwelling presence of the Holy Spirit. In earthly terms we might say that the Holy Spirit is CEO of God's government on the inside of you. The ministry of Jesus amply demonstrates the connection of the Holy Spirit and the kingdom. For example, in Matthew 12:28 Jesus said, "But if I cast out demons by the Spirit of God, surely the kingdom of God has come upon you." Likewise, when Jesus sent out the twelve apostles to "heal the sick, cleanse the lepers, raise the dead, cast out demons," He also instructed them to "preach, saying, 'The kingdom of heaven is at hand'" (Matthew 10:7-8). The demonstration of the power of the Holy Spirit is the manifestation of the presence of the Kingdom of God. Without that power, there is no possibility of advancing the Kingdom, as clearly shown in the charge that Jesus gave to the apostles prior to His ascension (Acts 1:1-8). For 40 days He had taught them "of the things pertaining to the kingdom of God." Now, in no uncertain terms, He commands them to stay in Jerusalem to await "the Promise of the Father" concerning the baptism with the Holy Spirit, when they would receive power to accomplish the mission to which He had appointed them.

There is no Kingdom apart from the Holy Spirit. Everything in the Kingdom operates under His influence. Without him the Kingdom of God cannot function or even exist, any more than a car can run without a battery, or a ship can cruise across the ocean without a rudder. Jesus tells us in John 14:15-17, 26 that it is only through the Holy Spirit that we live in the Kingdom. He comes from God the Father to live in us and be our Governor. The Holy Spirit is here to guide us and lead us into all the truth of the Kingdom of God.

The Truth

After Jesus described His Kingdom as not of this world, Pilate asked Him again, "Are you a king?" Jesus responded: "You say rightly that I am a king. For this cause I was born, and for this cause I have come into the world, that I should bear witness to the truth. Everyone who is of the truth hears My voice" (John 18:37). Jesus said that if His kingdom were of the world, His followers would use worldly methods as their weapons. But He said that the only weapon He used to attract people to the Kingdom is the weapon of the truth.

The Time of the Kingdom

When is the Kingdom of God coming? Jesus announced its arrival, but was He speaking of the coming of the Kingdom as a future reality, or as something that was actually present in His earthly ministry? The place to seek the answer is the New Testament.

The Present

Several passages of Scripture seem to indicate clearly the presence of the Kingdom during the ministry of Jesus. In Mark 1:15, Jesus proclaimed, "The time is fulfilled, and the kingdom of God is at hand." Although some may argue that "at hand" isn't quite the same as "is here," the Greek phrase gives the sense of something urgent already taking place. In fact, the phrase "at hand" explains the first part of the statement, "the time is fulfilled." The word "time" here is not ordinary calendar time. It's God's providential time. Jesus is saying, "This is the moment, the appointed time." The word "fulfilled" refers to the many prophecies that had been made. The coming of Jesus has brought them to pass. The time was fulfilled because the Kingdom of God was at hand. And the Kingdom of God was at hand because the King had arrived.

In Matthew 12:28 Jesus responded to those who had accused Him of casting out demons with the power of the devil: "But if I cast out demons by the Spirit of God, surely the kingdom of God has come upon you." The true source of His authority was the Spirit of God, and that fact is evidence that the Kingdom of God is already present. Moreover, the Greek verb translated "has come" is in the past tense (aorist), meaning that the Kingdom of God has already come.

In Luke 17:21 Jesus told the Pharisees that they could realize that the Kingdom of God was right there "among them," or "in their midst" by the works He was doing. For a fuller discussion of this verse, go back to the paragraph entitled "The Kingdom Is Not Merely in Our Hearts."

Colossians 1:13 says, "He has delivered us from the power of darkness and conveyed us into the kingdom of the Son of His love." This statement indicates that the Kingdom is already present.

The Future

There are other passages that indicate that the Kingdom still lies in the future. For example, Jesus taught us to pray, "Your kingdom come. Your will be done on earth as it is in heaven" (Matthew 6:10). The implication is that God's Kingdom is not present now, but it is a future happening. Another statement of Jesus in Matthew 8:11-12 points to a future Kingdom: "And I say to you that many will come from east and west and sit down with Abraham, Isaac, and Jacob in the kingdom of heaven. But the sons of the kingdom will be cast out into outer darkness. There will be weeping and gnashing of teeth." This statement has to do with believing Gentiles and unbelieving Jews. "Sons of the kingdom" was a term for the nation of Israel. The Jews believed that the Kingdom was meant only for Israel, but Jesus showed that merely being born into Israel doesn't automatically guarantee a place in the Kingdom. Note that many "will come," indicating that they have not yet arrived.

In Luke 19:11 Jesus "spoke another parable, because He was near Jerusalem and because they thought the kingdom of God would appear immediately." In other words, they thought that Jesus was going to Jerusalem to fulfill their expectations about driving out the Romans and setting up an earthly kingdom. But Jesus told a parable about a nobleman going "into a far country to receive for himself a kingdom and to return," making it clear that the Kingdom is not coming the way they thought. The point is that Jesus is going back to heaven and will be gone for some time before He returns to establish His Kingdom in power and glory.

At the Last Supper Jesus said, "I will not drink of this fruit of the vine from now on until that day when I drink it new with you in My Father's kingdom" (Matthew 26:29). In this statement He was looking ahead to the time when He will share in the messianic banquet with His disciples.

Already and Not Yet

These texts that we have quoted, as well as many others, clearly indicate that the Kingdom of God was already present during the earthly ministry of Jesus, but at the same time, in a sense, it was still in the future. A simple way of describing it is to say that the Kingdom is already here, but it has not been consummated, or to put it another way, it has not yet reached its fullness. Through His death on the cross, Jesus has provided for our deliverance "from this present evil age" (Galatians 1:4), but not yet has every knee bowed to the Lord Jesus (Philippians 2:10). Jesus has won the victory, but rebellion against Him continues. Death, suffering, persecution, and all kinds of evil are still present on the earth. In Revelation 6:10 those who have been killed because of their faith ask when God will execute judgment and avenge their blood. The answer is, "Not yet. Judgment is already confirmed. It's certain and it's coming but wait a little while" (Revelation 6:11).

Several parables of Jesus indicate that the Kingdom already is here, but it has not yet come in fullness. For example, the Kingdom is like a mustard seed that starts out small, but eventually "becomes greater than all herbs" (Mark 4:32). The Kingdom arrived in Jesus not in an overnight military coup, but like an infinitesimal seed destined for greatness. Like yeast in bread dough, the Kingdom at present may seem insignificant, but it will multiply and spread and permeate the whole batch (Matthew 13:33). The Kingdom grows gradually like a seed planted in the ground grows until the harvest (Mark 4:26-29).

So, we live in this in-between time, and the Kingdom of God is the essence of the Church's message and life. We are called to the Kingdom's life and power in the present, while still anticipating its final fullness and consummation in the future. Although presently limited in its scope and effects, the Kingdom really has arrived. The King has come. He has won the victory. He has dealt with sin once and for all by His self-sacrifice on the cross. He has all authority. He sits at the Father's right hand and reigns now until all His enemies are under His feet. The King's righteousness is now already ours by faith. His peace and joy have already been given to us. His Spirit is now already dwelling in us, transforming us into the King's character enabling us to walk in victory and holiness, empowering us to bear witness to Him, and granting us authority over all the power of the enemy. The yeast is spreading. The gospel of the Kingdom is being preached as a testimony to all nations (Matthew 24:14). Then the King will return, and the world will see Him "coming in the clouds with great power and glory" (Mark 13:26). The "not yet" will become the "already."

PROCLAIMING THE KINGDOM

We have seen that the central message of Jesus was "the kingdom of God is at hand" (Mark 1:15). This Kingdom was not a physical territory where God reigns, but rather the reign of God itself. It's God's rule, authority, and power, where His will is as perfectly done on earth as it is in heaven. All through His ministry, that reign was the emphasis of Jesus. But how did He convey that message? What means did He use?

Preaching

The simplest and most basic way that Jesus declared the message of the Kingdom was to preach it. There was no gospel of the Kingdom to proclaim until Christ arrived. Now that He has come, however, the Good News of the Kingdom must be preached to all, especially to the poor (Lk. 4:18,19; 7:22). The preaching of the Kingdom points people to the Kingdom itself. We are told, "After John was put in prison, Jesus came to Galilee, preaching the gospel of the kingdom of God" (Mark 1:14). The word that is translated as "preaching" (*kerysso*) was not a word confined to announcing the gospel. In fact, it was a very common word in the Roman Empire, used for an official proclamation. In this sense, the word "heralding" would be a better translation. The messenger of the news was called a "herald," an official spokesman commissioned by the emperor or government. His specific assignment was to announce with a clear and unquestionable voice whatever message the emperor or government entrusted to express to proclaim to the people. This word conveys several notions and ideas that will help us to understand its significance.

First, there was a note of *certainty*. The herald did not go out to the public square, blow his trumpet, and say, "I don't have all the facts yet, and I don't quite know what's going on, or what's going to take place, but I hope that something's going to happen." That is not heralding! The herald was speaking on behalf of the king, and there was no room for mistakes or ambiguities in his delivery of the message. A herald had a definite, concrete, specific message. He would blow his trumpet and shout, "I have an official statement from the emperor to declare to you!"

There was a note of *authority* in the word. This message was issued by the king, and it carried the weight of the highest authenticity. It wasn't the case of a man gathering a crowd and giving his own opinion about what has happened or what may happen. He had in his hand a document with the royal seal, and there was no question that this message was an absolute unequivocal statement, and no one could question it.

There was a note of *finality* in the word. As the king's spokesman, the herald had no right to speak his own mind, give his own personal commentary about what the king meant, or draw any attention to himself. He proclaimed the exact message given to him, nothing more, nothing less. He did not add to it, take from it, or change it in any way to make it more palatable to his listeners. When he stood before the people to announce the message given to him, it had to be accurate, precise, and faithful to what the king wanted to express to his people.

Explanations

The New Testament doesn't contain a thematic outline of the teachings of Jesus about the Kingdom of God, but He often gave provocative explanations of some features of the Kingdom. Mark 10:14-15 provides an example: "Let the little children come to Me, and do not forbid them; for of such is the kingdom of God. Assuredly, I say to you, whoever does not receive the kingdom of God as a little child will be no means enter it." The point of this statement, that we must receive the Kingdom in a childlike manner, provides some information about the Kingdom of God. There is the suggestion of the kind of faith and humility that we are to have. Instead of seeking to gain entrance into the Kingdom of God through our own efforts or merit, we must realize that in relation to entering the Kingdom, we are as helpless and dependent as children. There is no room in the Kingdom for those who have an exalted opinion of themselves, or who think they will gain eternal life through their wisdom or good works. Children are utterly dependent on their parents, and they have a simple complete trust that their parents will care for them. No one will receive the Kingdom of God without this helpless dependence and lowly humility.

Parables

One of the most common methods Jesus employed in communicating His message was the use of parables, some of which we shared earlier. A parable is basically a brief and simple story that illustrates a moral or spiritual lesson. On one occasion the disciples of Jesus asked Him, "Why do you speak to them in parables?" His response sounds somewhat bewildering, as though His intention was to confuse people. He answered, "Because it has been given to you to know the mysteries of the kingdom of heaven, but to them it has not been given." Contrary to what some people may think, His purpose in teaching in parables, not only those concerning the Kingdom, but other topics as well, was not to withhold truth from people, but to enlighten earnest listeners and seekers. If you examine carefully the teaching methods of Jesus, you will discover that He hardly ever answered a direct question. Usually, He would turn the question around, and He would present His teaching in such a way that it separated genuine seekers of truth from insincere pretenders who had no real interest in hearing the truth. So, Jesus told parables not to keep people from understanding, but to act as sort of a sieve to filter out those with wrong attitudes and motives. Receiving truth is as much a matter of the heart as well as the head. Casual listeners or those interested only in debate or criticism would rarely get past the external features of a parable, missing the real point altogether. By way of explanation to His disciples, Jesus quoted Isaiah 6:9-10: "Hearing you will hear and shall not understand, and seeing you will see and not perceive; for the hearts of this people have grown dull" (Matthew 13:14-15). It was not that God was deliberately hiding the truth from them. They had the opportunity to believe, but they did not want to hear. Those who were sincere in following Jesus would understand the parables and thus comprehend the great truths of the Kingdom of God.

The Works of Jesus

Jesus proclaimed God's coming reign not only in words, but also in works. He did more than preach the Kingdom; He demonstrated its reality with "signs of the Kingdom," public evidence that the Kingdom He was talking about had come. His deeds both illustrated the Kingdom of God and demonstrated its presence. Without these works that gave credence to His words, Jesus' announcement of the Kingdom would have had no impact on His listeners. People would have regarded Him as a self-centered dreamer, as a deliberate deceiver, or as a demonically driven imposter. They would certainly not have received His claim to have been divinely sent as the envoy of the Kingdom. A miracle is a happening beyond human capacity to do or prevent, and which only God can do or prevent. It is God doing what only God can do. It is God building that which cannot be built and God destroying that which cannot be destroyed. The miracles of Jesus are dramatic defilements of the laws of nature that demonstrate His power and authority over all creation. Blind and deaf people don't suddenly start seeing and hearing; dead people don't come back to life; deformed bodies don't instantly straighten themselves; a fish and bread lunch doesn't multiply itself. When we discern God's hand in events outside the ordinary course of nature, we see miracles. There are different categories of miracles— exorcisms, physical healings, the raising of the dead, and nature miracles, such as calming a storm, turning water into wine, shriveling a fig tree, multiplying fish and bread, and walking on water.

The miracles were not the main event nor the main purpose of God's actions. They are rather signs along the road to help keep us journeying toward the Kingdom of God. The signs exist to keep us on the right track by reminding us of God's Kingdom and to keep us alert and watchful for what direction we are to take.

In the feeding of the 5000, the people asked Jesus, "What shall we do, that we may work the works of God?" Jesus answered and said to them, "This is the work of God, that you believe in Him whom He sent."

Healings

The healings of Jesus demonstrated His authority over disease, sickness, and death, but they did more than reveal Him as a compassionate teacher. They were signs of the presence of God's reign on earth, as the prophets foretold. For example, Isaiah 35 contains a prophecy of God coming to save and redeem His people. The following promise is found in the context of that prophecy: "Then the eyes of the blind shall be opened, and the ears of the deaf shall be unstopped. Then the lame shall leap like a deer, and the tongue of the dumb sing (Isaiah 35:5-6). The ministry of Jesus fulfilled this promise, proving the presence of the kingdom. Jesus Himself pointed to His healings as evidence of the coming of the Kingdom. When John the Baptist sent some of his disciples to ask Jesus if He indeed was the One who had come to bring the Kingdom, He responded: "Go and tell John the things which you hear and see. The blind see and the lame walk; the lepers are cleansed and the deaf hear; the dead are raised up and the poor have the gospel preached to them" (Matthew 11:2-5). Essentially, Jesus was telling John to compare His ministry to the promise of Isaiah concerning healings. There can be only one conclusion—Jesus is the One through whom the Kingdom has come.

Casting out Demons

Since "for this purpose the Son of God was manifested, that He might destroy the works of the devil" (1 John 3:8), Jesus inevitably came into collision with the prince of darkness. At the very beginning of His ministry, there was an attempt by spiritual forces to hinder God's redemptive plan. Satan tried to tempt Jesus into sin, which would have disqualified Him from being the Savior of humanity. Throughout the rest of His ministry Jesus had many encounters with demonic beings, and central to His ministry was delivering people from the clutches of those powers. The Gospels record several specific occasions on which Jesus cast out evil spirits (see Matthew 8:32; 12:22; Mark 1:25; 5:8; 9:25; 7:26; 16:9; Luke 4:35; 8:29; 11:14), and there are other references to casting out many demons. For example, Mark 1:39 says, "He was preaching in their synagogues throughout all Galilee, and casting out demons" (see Matthew 8:16; Luke 4:41; 13:32). Casting out demons demonstrated the power and authority of Jesus over the spiritual world and gave clear evidence of the presence of the Kingdom. The devil was retreating before the advance of the King. As Jesus put it, once the strong man has been overpowered by the Stronger One, his possessions can be taken from him (Luke 11:22; Matthew 12:29).

In Matthew 12:24 some of the Pharisees accused Jesus of casting out demons with the power of Beelzebub, another name for the devil. He answered them first by showing the absurdity of the charge: "Every kingdom divided against itself is brought to desolation, and every city or house divided against itself will not stand" (Matthew 12:25). Then he added, "But if I cast out demons by the Spirit of God, surely the kingdom of God has come upon you" (Matthew 12:28). Luke 11:20 records this statement of Jesus: "But if I cast out demons with the finger of God, surely the kingdom of God has come upon you." By this statement, Jesus was declaring that God's kingly power and authority were present to overthrow the work of Satan in order to restore things as God intended them to be—here "on earth, as it is in heaven."

Nature Miracles

The miracles of Jesus are a major part of His ministry. Their prominence was such that even His enemies had to acknowledge that He was a miracle worker, even though they challenged the authority with which He performed them. The accounts of the miracles of Jesus were not recorded simply to recount the factual details of His marvelous actions. Rather, they were reported as powerful signs of the presence of the Kingdom of God and testimony to Jesus as the proclaimer and embodiment of God's Kingdom. In those miracles God was acting, as Jesus Himself testified (see Matthew 12:28). The Greek word *semeion*, translated as "sign," is used 17 times in the Gospel of John to describe the miracles of Jesus. John declared that the mighty deeds that Jesus performed were signs that "manifested His glory" (John 2:11), as well as the power of God working through Him. The miracles were not an end in themselves, intended to amaze people. While they served to meet an immediate need, they also served as "signs" pointing to a greater reality. Acts 2:22 declares that Jesus of Nazareth was "a man attested by God to you by miracles, wonders and signs which God did through Him." The miracles substantiated the claims of Jesus to be the Son of God and testified to the fact that the Kingdom of God was breaking forth in the world.

Signs, then, are evidence of the message and establishment of the Kingdom of God. Jesus sent His disciples out "to preach the kingdom of God and to heal the sick" (Luke 9:2), and they did. In the Book of Acts, we read that they did the same mighty works that Jesus did, and more, just as Jesus promised (John 14:12-14). The apostle Paul wrote, "My speech and my preaching were not with persuasive words of human wisdom but in demonstration of the Spirit and of power" (1 Corinthians 2:4). Jesus assured the disciples that miraculous signs will follow the preaching of the gospel (Mark 16:16). How is it possible to perform the same mighty works of Jesus? It's because Jesus did so by the Spirit of God, and the same Spirit works through His disciples. In

His earthly ministry Jesus ministered by the power of the Word and the power of the Spirit, just as His disciples can do, with the difference being that Jesus did not have to contend with the hindrances of sin. Jesus was fully human, yet without sin, and at the same time He was fully divine. During His time on earth, He did not rely on His divine capacities (omniscience, omnipotence, and omnipresence) to exercise His ministry, indicating that by the power of the Holy Spirit, we can expect to see signs and miracles in our own ministry.

LIVING IN THE KINGDOM

The Bible makes it very clear that there is a vast difference between the lifestyle of the Kingdom of God and the lifestyle of the kingdom of the world. The contrast is as striking as that of day and night, life and death, freedom and bondage, purity and corruption. The Old Testament declares the uniqueness of Israel, most often by the word "holy," which means "different," "set apart," "separated," and "distinct." The New Testament applies the same description to followers of Jesus Christ, and they demonstrate their distinctiveness in every situation of life. God's people are to be holy because God is holy (1 Peter 1:14-16). They are "a holy nation, His own special people," having been set apart by God to be exclusively His, to be dedicated to Him, and to manifest holiness of heart and conduct in contrast to the impurity of non-citizens of the Kingdom of God (1 Peter 2:9-12).

Entering the Kingdom

With Jesus came the arrival of a Kingdom made up of men and women who are totally committed to doing the will of God. That Kingdom is completely different from the kingdoms of this world because it *is* different. It demands holiness, a moral commitment from those who follow Him. That's a crucial point that forever separates the Kingdom of God from every earthly kingdom. Being in an earthly kingdom is merely a matter of geography. You are a citizen of whatever place where you experienced birth. That's not the way it is with the Kingdom of God. As Jesus said to Pilate, "Everyone who is of the truth hears me" (John 18:37). The Kingdom of God is reserved for those who recognize and follow the truth as it is revealed in Jesus Christ. There can be no rejection of or neutrality concerning the things that Jesus taught.

As we have seen, we are living in a tolerant age that embraces an inclusivism that automatically grants practically everyone a passport to heaven, regardless of their beliefs or disbeliefs. Such a perspective is a blank contradiction to the plain teachings of the Bible, where there is nothing vague or indefinite about entrance into the Kingdom of God. A person is either in it or outside it. Jesus once said to a man, "You are not far from the kingdom of God" (Mark 12:34). The man was not in it; he was outside it. The Bible makes it very clear that the choice of whether to enter or to remain outside is entirely up to the individual. There is a gate of entry into the Kingdom, and Jesus described it as a "narrow gate" (Matthew 7:13). It isn't a broad and wide gate where people can sneak through or stumble their way in unintentionally. No one has ever become a citizen of the Kingdom by accident and unawares. Becoming a citizen of the Kingdom is a matter of choice, and it demands a definite decision. Moses stated it this way: "I call heaven and earth as witnesses today against you, that I have set before you life and death, blessing and cursing; therefore choose life" (Deuteronomy 30:19). Joshua also presented the people with a definite choice: "Choose for yourselves this day whom you will serve" (Joshua 24:15). Lot's wife could not make up her mind between following God or staying in a wicked environment, and disaster overcame her (Genesis 19:26). Using her indecision as an example, Jesus warned, "Remember Lot's wife" (Luke 17:32). A man expressed to Jesus his desire to follow Him, but first he wanted to go home and spend some time there. In response, Jesus said, "No one, having put his hand to the plow, and looking back, is fit for the kingdom of God" (Luke 9:61-62).

A New Birth

Jesus used the phrase "entering the kingdom" many times, and in doing so, He gave clear instructions concerning the way to become a citizen of the Kingdom of God. The most thorough unequivocal teaching that He gave was in His dramatic interview with Nicodemus, recorded in John 3. Here is the plainest and final answer to the question, "How can I enter the Kingdom of God?" It's essential to note that Jesus repeatedly prefaced His remarks with the words "amen, amen," variously translated as "verily, verily," "truly, truly," "most assuredly," or "I guarantee you" (verses 3, 5, 11). That formula is always followed by the pronouncement of something of weighty seriousness and deep importance. Jesus used the words to denote the absolute truthfulness, validity, and stamp of final divine authority on what He says. He was declaring that whatever human opinion may be concerning the subject, His word is the only one that matters because He *is* the Truth.

Three times in the conversation, Jesus spoke the key phrase that gives entrance to the Kingdom: "Born again!" (Verses 3, 5, 7). Some commentators translate this crucial phrase as "born from above." Others say it should be translated as "born anew." We must bear in mind that Jesus was likely conversing with Nicodemus in Aramaic, which was translated into Greek, and then into English from the Greek. The original statement in Aramaic means, "If a person is not born again, it is impossible for that one to see the Kingdom of God." The question of Nicodemus in verse 4 gives evidence that Jesus was talking about another birth. All the phrases actually denote the same thing— "born again," "born from above," "born anew," "born of the Spirit," and "another birth"—so take your choice.

The important thing is that there is both a negative and a positive meaning in the doctrine of a new birth. Negatively, being born again is not just an amendment or addition to something you already are. In other words, entering the Kingdom of God involves more than a reformation of or a little improvement on what you were before. The statement of Nicodemus in verse 2 indicates that although he was "a ruler of the Jews," he wanted whatever Jesus had that was extra and new. The response of Jesus was, "You can't add anything to what you are. You must start over. You are dead, not living, and you must be born again."

Positively, to enter the Kingdom of God we need a completely new start, comparable to being born again. The New Testament sometimes calls the new birth "a new creation" or "regeneration." Regeneration is a radical rebirth and transformational change. It means that what you are by nature is barren and hopeless, and you need to be a new person with a new nature. You were dead; you need life. In regeneration, God does not renovate us or improve us to make us a little better. Regeneration is the spiritual transformation in a person, brought about by the Holy Spirit that brings the individual from being spiritually dead to become spiritually alive. The new birth is a resurrection, a new life, a new creature conceived by the Holy Spirit. It is a dying to sin and living to righteousness, a translation from darkness to light. We are made "partakers of the divine nature" (2 Peter 1:4). The Bible says, "If anyone is in Christ, he is a new creation; old things have passed away; behold, all things have become new" (2 Corinthians 5:17). A person who has been born again has a new outlook and understanding; he has new desires and ambitions; he has a new lifestyle. In short, he is a new creation, with a completely new start.

It's significant that in addressing Nicodemus, Jesus used the all-embracing phrase "unless one," meaning anyone. It doesn't matter what person you are talking about, whether it's a highly respected religious leader such as Nicodemus, or the refuse of society such as the Publicans, or the lowly open sinners such as prostitutes and criminals. The point is that there is no exception to the necessity of being born again in order to enter the Kingdom of God.

But why is it necessary to be born again, especially for morally upright people who live decent lives and do good works? The first reason is that we were born with a sinful nature. Regeneration is necessary because all descendants of Adam and Eve have inherited their sinful nature and are morally unable to do what is good. The Bible teaches in Ephesians 2:1-9 that people are by nature dead in trespasses and sins. In this state, they are without God and without hope in the world. Not in response to their merit, but freely and in love, God speaks the word that raises the dead. The world's idea is that if you just straighten yourself up, reform yourself from a few bad habits, and practice good works, then you are okay. That is not biblical Christianity. It may be morality or ethical behavior, but it is far removed from Christianity.

Apart from the new birth, there is no understanding of spiritual truth. The Bible teaches in 2 Corinthians 2:6-16 that no person can comprehend the things of God without the illumination of the Holy Spirit. "But the natural man does not receive the things of the Spirit of God, for they are foolishness to him; nor can he know them, because they are spiritually discerned" (2 Corinthians 2:14). In other words, spiritual things can be understood only by spiritual people, who have experienced the new birth through the Holy Spirit. Nicodemus was well-taught in the Scriptures and an expert on the Jewish religion, yet he was bewildered by what Jesus had to say (John 3:4, 9). He thought that Jesus was talking about a literal second physical birth. Jesus explained his lack of understanding by pointing out that his thinking was limited to the physical realm. Because he dwelt only in the flesh and did not have a spiritual birth, Nicodemus could not think in spiritual categories (John 3:5-12). He was like a person born deaf trying to understand music, or like a person born blind trying to critique art.

It's the same with modern men and women who have not experienced a new birth. They have no comprehension when confronted with spiritual truth. They may be highly educated experts in their field of learning; they may be clever thinkers; they may possess high intellectual acumen, but they are totally incapable of understanding the truths of God's Word because their nature is wrong. Not only do they lack spiritual understanding, but "the carnal mind is enmity against God; for it is not subject to the law of God, nor indeed can be" (Romans 8:7). Jesus explained it quite clearly in John 3:19: "This is the condemnation, that the light has come into the world, and men loved darkness rather than light, because their deeds were evil." These statements explain the turmoil, confusion, and evil in the world. They explain why people openly celebrate practices that are offensive to God and condemned in His Word. "That which is born of the flesh is flesh" (John 3:6), and it is at enmity with God, and it will never rise above its own level and its own nature. That's why we need to be born again.

There is a second reason for the necessity of the new birth. We need to be born again not only because of what we are in our old unredeemed nature but because of the nature of the Kingdom of God. We have seen that it is not a physical, external kingdom; it is something spiritual. It is not a moral code of rules and regulations. It is not a matter of rites and ceremonies, or transcendental meditation, or philosophical cogitation. It is entering into a personal relationship with God. It means a fellowship with God, with the enjoyment of a spiritual communion in which you speak to Him and He speaks to you. You live in the realm of the spiritual, in which the original relationship between God and Adam and Eve is restored and you have companionship with God.

But how is such a relationship possible? By being born again! The Bible tells us in 2 Corinthians 6:14-16: "Do not be unequally yoked together with unbelievers. For what fellowship has righteousness with lawlessness? And what communion has light with darkness? And what accord has Christ with Belial? Or what part has a believer with an unbeliever? And what agreement has the temple of God with idols? For you are the temple of the living God. As God has said: 'I will dwell in them and walk among them. I will be their God, and they shall be My people.'"

That is what it means to be in the Kingdom of God, but before we can enter it, we must have something in us that corresponds to it. That is why we need to be born again. In response to the bewilderment of Nicodemus, Jesus in effect said, "I have talked to you about earthly things, and you haven't believed. How will you believe if I tell you heavenly things? I'm not talking to you about things you can learn with your own natural intellect. I'm telling you spiritual things that are beyond your natural understanding, and you must be born again and have a renewed mind before you can understand" (John 3:9-13). Jesus went on to explain to Nicodemus how He came to earth to bear the punishment of sin, and that the only way of salvation was to believe in Him (John 3:14-21). But that message of the cross was and still is foolishness to those who don't believe (1 Corinthians 1:18-23). To summarize, the teaching of the Kingdom is that men and women can be regenerated, born again, and have a new nature. They can start anew and receive a new life. The natural person cannot receive that message; therefore, there is the need to be born again.

But how can a person be born again? Jesus explained that it's a great mystery because it's a miracle, the birth of the Spirit. At the beginning of the Gospel of John, we see that the new birth is the great act of God. John explains how Jesus came into the world as the true Light, but His own people rejected Him. "But as many as received him, to them He gave the right to become children of God, to those who believe in His name: who were born, not of blood, nor of the will of the flesh, nor of the will of man, but of God" (John 1:12-13). The new nature can only be realized by the power of God.

Repentance

Are we to do nothing, then, except to wait passively for God to effect the new birth in us? Remember that when announcing the arrival of the Kingdom, Jesus gave the two-fold directive to repent and believe as requirements to enter the Kingdom (Mark 1:15). Repentance and faith always go together, and the order of the two is very important. Genuine repentance always comes before genuine faith. Without true repentance, there can be no saving faith. In this day of tolerance and compromise, while we still hear about faith, there is much less emphasis on the necessity of repentance. Not long ago I heard a pastor say that he no longer preaches about sin and judgment and the need to repent. His reason? "I don't want to offend anybody." The kind of shallow preaching that he and others do fits into the "other gospel" category, and their kind of religion is a counterfeit Christianity that ignores human sinfulness and guilt and the command for "all men everywhere to repent" (Acts 17:30-31). A gospel that offers salvation without repentance, and I might add, the necessity of a new birth, is no gospel at all, and it succeeds only in making people feel comfortable in their sins all the way to hell.

What is repentance? Before answering that question, let's first see what repentance is not.

Repentance is more than conviction of sin. It's possible to feel conviction and still not repent. Felix trembled with conviction under Paul's preaching, but he didn't repent (Acts 24:25).

Repentance is more than an acknowledgement of sin. In true repentance outward confession is matched by a change on the inside. There are many examples in the Bible of people acknowledging the fact that they have sinned, but they didn't repent. In Exodus 9:27, after God brought hail and fire on Egypt, Pharaoh said, "I have sinned," but in Exodus 9:34, "When Pharaoh saw that the rain, the hail, and the thunder had ceased, he sinned yet more, and he hardened his heart." When things got better, he went right back to what he was doing.

The hypocritical prophet Balaam wanted to serve God and at the same time make a profit by betraying God's people. In Numbers 22:34 he confessed, "I have sinned," but he did not change.

King Saul disobeyed God's command by keeping some of the spoils of war. When the prophet Samuel confronted him, the king said, "I have sinned. . .because I feared the people and obeyed their voice" (1

Samuel 15:24). He confessed his sin, but instead of repenting, he made an excuse.

In the battle of Jericho, Achan disobeyed God by stashing away some treasures of the city. When confronted by Joshua, he acknowledged, "Indeed I have sinned against the Lord God of Israel" (Joshua 7:20). He was sorry, not for his sin, but for getting caught.

After he betrayed Jesus, Judas expressed remorse, but not repentance when he said, "I have sinned by betraying innocent blood" (Matthew 7:3-4).

Feeling conviction of sin, acknowledging it, and being regretful are related to repentance, but that is not the meaning of the word. To repent literally means "to change one's mind," with the understanding that the change of mind leads to a change of action. For example, if you are driving on a highway and suddenly realize that you are going in the wrong direction, you will stop, turn around, and head in the opposite direction. You have repented, that is, you have changed your mind about the direction in which you should be going, and you have turned around. But if you realize that you're going in the wrong direction and decide to keep going without turning around, you have not really repented. By your failure to act, you have shown that even though you know you are wrong, you feel just fine with the way you're going.

In the New Testament, there is a negative and a positive action involved in repentance. In Acts 20:21 Paul preached "repentance toward God and faith toward our Lord Jesus Christ." In the biblical sense, repentance is a turning from sin and a turning to Jesus. When you repent, you recognize that your sin is offensive to God, and you do a complete about-face and turn from sin and self to God. From various references in the Bible, we can see four elements in repentance.

When you truly repent, you *become aware* of your own guilt, sinfulness, and helplessness (Psalm 51:4-10; 109:21-22).

When you truly repent, you *reach out* for God's mercy in Jesus Christ (Psalm 51:1; 130:4). Repentance allows God's grace to work in your heart.

When you truly repent, you *change* your attitude and actions concerning sin. You turn from sin to God (Psalm 119:128; Job 42:5-6; 2 Corinthians 7:10). You cannot cling to your sin and to Jesus at the same time.

When you truly repent, you radically and persistently *pursue* a life of holiness and obedience (2 Timothy 2:19-22; 1 Peter 1:16). Repentance is not something you do once in order to get saved and then forget it. Repentance is an act followed by a process.

Faith

The words "believe" and "faith" are translations of the same Greek word. Repentance and faith are two sides of the same coin. It's impossible to place your faith in Jesus Christ as Savior and Lord without first changing your mind about sin and about who Jesus is and what He has done. Biblical repentance, in relation to salvation, is changing your mind from rejection of Christ to faith in Christ. Faith focuses on Jesus and His redemptive work, not on your own efforts. To simplify biblical faith as it relates to salvation, we might analyze it as having three parts—knowing, agreeing, and committing.

Faith is not a blind leap into the dark unknown. It's based on facts that you learn from the Bible about Jesus and what He has done to save sinners. Romans 10:17 tells us, "Faith comes by hearing, and hearing by the word of God."

The second step of faith is when you accept as truth the facts that you have learned about Jesus. You reach this point because of the convicting power of the Holy Spirit, who "will guide you into all truth" (John 16:13).

The third part of faith is when you make your conviction that Jesus is Lord and Savior a personal matter by wholeheartedly committing yourself to Him and surrendering to His lordship over your life.

Let me illustrate this process. Suppose you are on a hike, and you come to a bridge over a wide and deep gorge. You hesitate to step out on the bridge because you're not convinced that it's sturdy enough to hold your weight. But as you watch and wait, you see all kinds of traffic cross the bridge—pedestrians, some with heavy packs; people on horseback; bicycles; and motorcycles. By your observation, you know that the bridge can hold heavy weights, and you become convinced that it's safe for you to cross. But your knowledge and your conviction will not get you across the chasm. You must actively commit yourself to stepping out onto the bridge and entrust yourself totally to the strength of the bridge. You don't walk in different directions to seek any other way across; you don't try to jump across; you don't try to use a pole vault; you don't try to swing across; you don't try to go down this side of the gorge, swim across the stream, and then scale the other side. You are convinced that there is no other way, so you take a step of faith and rely completely on the bridge.

That's how it is with biblical faith. You can know about Jesus and His mission on earth to sacrifice Himself for your sins, and you are convinced by the Holy Spirit that the gospel is true. You believe that Jesus is the Son of God, that He died on the cross for sinners, that He defeated the grave three days later, that He ascended to heaven, and that He will return one day. You believe John 3:18: "He who believes in Him is not condemned; but he who does not believe is condemned already, because he has not believed in the name of the only begotten Son of

God." However, believing is more than mental assent. One step remains. You renounce all other supposed methods of salvation. You don't rely on your own efforts, and you don't entrust yourself to any teaching that promises you another way. You repent and by faith place your life in the hands of Jesus, yielding to Him as your Savior and Lord.

When you are born again, having repented and yielded in faith to Jesus Christ, then you are welcomed into the kingdom of God.

Hindrances to Entering the Kingdom

What sets the gospel apart from any other message of faith is the simplicity of how we are welcomed into the Kingdom. The gospel presents the unconditional, unrelenting love of God that sent Jesus into the world to die for sinners and welcomes all who accept Him. Jesus encountered all kinds of people during His ministry—poor people, rich people, diseased people, self-righteous people, outcasts, prostitutes, thieves, socially ostracized people, oppressed people, religious snobs, agnostics, idolaters, religious pretenders, demoniacs. The way into the Kingdom of God was open to all these people, but various hindrances kept many from entering. We deal with the same obstacles today. Let's notice some of the most common ones.

Riches

The one barrier to the kingdom about which Jesus was most definite was the obstacle of riches. Mark 10 tells the story of a rich young ruler, upright in character and conduct, who preferred his wealth to eternity in heaven. After the young man had gone away sorrowfully, Jesus made a remarkable statement to His disciples: "How hard it is for those who have riches to enter the kingdom of God." Seeing the astonishment of the disciples, He elaborated: "It is easier for a camel to go through the eye of a needle than for a rich man to enter the kingdom of God" (Mark 10:17-27). In the parable of the sower, some seed was scattered among thorns, which then choked them as they sprouted. In His interpretation of the parable, Jesus revealed to His disciples that the thorns represent "the cares of this world and the deceitfulness of riches" (Matthew 13:22). The Bible insists that we should not "trust in uncertain riches but in the living God, who gives us richly all things to enjoy" (1 Timothy 6:17). Jesus said, "You cannot serve God and mammon" (Matthew 6:24). Mammon was a Hebrew word that stands for all wealth and all material things.

The Bible does not condemn the possession of riches. On the contrary, it shows that a wealthy person can do a great deal of good by the wise and generous use of his riches. For example, notice how God blessed Solomon with "both riches and honor" so that his wealth "surpassed all the kings of the earth in riches and wisdom" (1 Kings 3:13; 2 Chronicles 9:22). What is condemned is the spirit in people that causes them to put their trust in money, wealth, and possessions rather than in God. True faith in God acknowledges our complete dependence on Him, but the lure of wealth gives a false sense of security. Instead of looking to God as their provider, those who trust in wealth have the notion that they are the ruler of their own kingdom, that they are self-made, and that they are responsible for something that was done by God alone. In the case of the rich young ruler, Jesus wasn't so much concerned about his wealth as He was about the condition of his heart. His avaricious attitude toward his wealth prevented his devotion to Christ.

Self-righteousness

Self-righteous people are those who are so convinced of their own moral and spiritual superiority that they think they have no sin of which to repent. Usually, such people display a "holier-than-thou" attitude that judges and disdains others. In Luke 18:9-14 Jesus "spoke a parable to some who trusted in themselves that they were righteous, and despised others." It's the story of a Pharisee and a tax collector who went to the temple to pray. The Pharisee, by all appearances, was one of the most holy and devoted Jews around. Pharisees were extremely devout and highly disciplined in their religious practices. A Pharisee was obedient to the Law, even going above and beyond what the Law required, as this Pharisee informed God about himself.

The tax collector, on the other hand, was a very bad person in the view of Jewish society. Tax collectors were synonymous with traitors and cheats. They had sold out to the hated Roman oppressors, collecting the Roman tolls and padding their own pockets with whatever they wanted to charge over and above the required tax. The Romans overlooked this dishonesty as long they received their dues, but the Jews rightly considered the practice to be highly unethical and contrary to God's commands.

So here were two men coming before God in the temple, one at the top end of the righteousness ladder, and the other on the very bottom rung. The Pharisee was quite confident before God about himself and his own righteousness, and his prayer seems to be more of a braggadocio. The phrase, "prayed thus with himself," indicates that he was not praying to God at all. Rather, he was practically praying to himself, congratulating himself that he had no need to repent and pray for pardon. Even his very posture looks righteous as he begins to recite a hypocritical prayer of thanksgiving, which in fact was a proud recitation of the contrast between himself and rogues and thieves, and especially the miserable tax collector isolated in the corner.

The tax collector has such a burden for his sins that he can only beat his breast, utter a prayer of repentance, and ask for mercy. Consider the difference between the two prayers. In his prayer, the Pharisee uses the pronoun "I," making himself the subject of each sentence. He saw himself as holy because of what he did. In the tax collector's prayer, God is the subject, the one who shows mercy. The tax collector saw himself as a sinner, dependent on what God does, not on what he has done. The Pharisee made himself look better by comparing himself to sinners of low moral standards. The tax collector also made a comparison, but not to another person. He compared himself to the holiness of God, recognizing that he was far from righteous. The Pharisee believed that his acceptance by God was based on his own actions, whereas the tax collector recognized that there was nothing in himself that would cause God to approve of him and that his only hope was the grace of God.

The Pharisee went home from the temple the same way he came, righteous in his own eyes. Nothing had changed. But the tax collector experienced something different. He went home justified, that is, acquitted and declared righteous.

The New Testament strongly condemns self-righteousness, which is closely related to legalism, the idea that we can somehow generate within ourselves a righteousness that will be acceptable to God. Six times in Matthew 23, Jesus condemns the scribes and Pharisees for rigidly adhering to their legalistic traditions in order to gain acceptance before God and to make themselves look better to others. In Luke 5:31-32 Jesus made it clear that He can do nothing for those who think they are sinless and don't need God's forgiveness: "Those who are well have no need of a physician, but those who are sick." His ministry is for those who realize their need for repentance: "I have not come to call the righteous, but sinners, to repentance." He scathingly denounced self-righteousness as shutting the doors of the Kingdom of heaven (Matthew 23:13).

The Bible condemns the practice of seeking righteousness by

self-effort (Romans 2:17-24). Those who try to gain acceptance with God based on their own righteousness demonstrate ignorance of the true righteousness of God (Romans 10:3). Any teaching that leads people to believe that they can win acceptance with God by their own merit is a perversion of the true gospel, and those who teach it are accursed (Galatians 1:6-9). Furthermore, if righteousness comes by your own efforts, "then Christ died in vain" (Galatians 2:21).

Pride

The Bible clearly states that God hates pride (see Proverbs 6:17; 8:13; 16:5). Repeatedly we read that God brings down the haughty and the proud (see Psalm 18:27; 101:5; Isaiah 2:11; 5:15; Ezekiel 16:50; Amos 6:8). The Bible repeatedly warns against the dangers of arrogance (see Proverbs 16:18; 18:12). God actively opposes the proud (see James 4:6; 1 Peter 5:5). Pride is so abominable to God because it is a root sin, from which other evils sprout. Pride is like self-righteousness in that everything revolves around the proud person. To be arrogant is to be the center of your world and to look with disdain at others. There is little concern, if any, for what others think and no consideration of the will of God. Psalm 10:4 explains that the proud are so consumed with themselves that their thoughts are far from God. Pride sees no need for God, and the message of the cross is offensive to a person who does not even acknowledge that he is a sinner. God planned salvation as He did in order that no one can take credit for what He did through Christ (Ephesians 2:8-9). The proud, on the other hand, are so blinded by their pride that they think they have no need of God or, worse, that God should accept them as they are because they deserve His acceptance.

Worldliness

1 John 2:15 tells us that we are not to love the world, and James 4:4 tells us not to befriend the world. Yet John 3:16 speaks of God's overwhelming love for the world. So, if God loves the world, why are we forbidden to love the world? The answer is that while in the Bible the word "world" sometimes refers to the physical earth and universe (see John 13:1; Hebrews 1:2)), it also speaks of the world as a humanistic value system that is hostile to God (see Matthew 18:7; John 15:19; Romans 12:2; 1 John 4:5). Satan is the god of this world, and he has a corrupt value system completely opposed to God (John 14:30; 16:11; 2 Corinthians 4:4; Ephesians 2:2). The Bible summarizes Satan's value system in 1 John 2:16: "the lust of the flesh, the lust of the eyes, and the pride of life." These categories include every sin imaginable.

Therefore, when the Bible speaks of God's love for the world, it is referring to the people who inhabit the earth (1 John 4:9). Likewise, we are to love other people (Romans 13:8; 1 John 4:7; 1 Peter 1:22; et al). When the Bible tells us not to love the world, it's referring to the world's evil value system.

When we describe worldliness, we usually think of the more sordid examples of sinful behavior, especially the pursuits of pleasure. This concept is certainly true, and one of the saddest verses in the Bible is the plaintive statement of Paul, written in a Roman dungeon shortly before his death: "Demas has forsaken me, having loved this present world" (2 Timothy 4:10). But the list in 1 John 2:16 is more inclusive. Worldliness is adopting the world's thought patterns, attitudes, philosophies, and values. In short, it's preferring the world's priorities over God's value system. There is much to compete with God for our highest affection, and we can make an idol out of anything. Loving the world is idolatry (1 Corinthians 10:7, 14), and any passionate desire of our hearts that is not for God's glory can become an idol (1 Corinthians

10:31). Anyone who loves the world as unbelievers do is not fit for the Kingdom of God. How can anyone claim to believe the Bible and yet take the world's position on matters that the Bible explicitly addresses? I ask this question especially concerning those in places of church leadership, who are supposed to be spiritual guides, and yet who prefer public opinion over biblical pronouncements. A choice must be made when there is a direct conflict between the world's view and what God has decreed, and Jesus said that if we love anything more than Him, we are not worthy of Him (Matthew 10:37-38).

The new birth provides us an exit from the world's system (2 Corinthians 5:17; Colossians 1:13; Ephesians 2:1-6). We become citizens of another Kingdom (Philippians 3:20; Luke 12:32). We develop a heavenly mindset (Colossians 3:1-4) and our thinking becomes God-centered (Philippians 4:8-9). We see everything differently from the people of the world. Our priority is the kingdom of God, and we stop loving the world.

Delay

The invitation to enter the Kingdom of God can be refused, just as people may foolishly and discourteously refuse an invitation to be the guest at a feast (Matthew 22:1-14; Luke 14:15-24). Likewise, the inability to decide hinders people from entering the Kingdom of God. Some people, upon hearing the gospel and knowing their spiritual needs, delay in making a response. This is the most dangerous type of procrastination. Life is short, and we do not know what will happen tomorrow (James 4:14). The Bible urges us to get right with God today. "Today, if you will hear His voice, do not harden your hearts as in the rebellion" (Hebrews 3:15). The governor Felix came under great conviction when he heard the gospel from Paul, but he said, "Go away for now; when I have a convenient time I will call for you" (Acts 24:25). As far as we know that time never came. Later, King Agrippa also heard the gospel from Paul and was almost persuaded to become a Christian (Acts 26:28). Apparently, he never made the decision to become a disciple of Jesus. The opportunity to enter the Kingdom can be lost, just as the foolish bridesmaids lost their opportunity to share in the joy of the wedding festivities (Matthew 25:1-13). The privilege of entering the Kingdom may be taken away, as Jesus warned those who had consistently spurned the messengers of God, and those whose reaction to Him was without faith and without love (Matthew 21:43; 8:11; Luke 13:28). It is presumptuous and dangerous to impose on God's patient mercy.

The Priority of the Kingdom

Life in modern times makes many demands on our time and attention, and our lives can easily become cluttered and frazzled. Jesus said, "But seek first the kingdom of God and His righteousness, and all these things shall be added to you" (Matthew 6:33). If you read the verses leading up to this one, you will see that Jesus had been teaching about the cares, worries, and demands of life. While there are many things that seem so important as to demand our time and attention, there is only one thing that, to which if we give priority, will take care of all other demands and unclutter our lives.

The word "seek" means to "actively pursue," to "go after," to "aim at," or to "strive after." In Matthew 6:33 it's a present, active imperative verb, which means a continuous or habitual seeking. Every day of your life you are to make the daily choice of prioritizing God's kingdom and righteousness. The word "first" translates a Greek word that has two meanings. It means first in a succession of things, that is, something that is number one on a list of things. The word also means first in the sense of having the most significance, being the most prominent, and deserving primary focus. Both meanings are present in this verse. Jesus is teaching that nothing is as important as the Kingdom of God, and there is nothing that we should put before the Kingdom of God. The Kingdom should be the obsession of your life. As we have seen, a kingdom is a place where a king rules, so to seek the Kingdom of God is to seek the rule and the reign of God over your entire life, completely subject to His commands and instructions. In God's Kingdom you don't get a voice, a vote, or a veto. You are to live your life in absolute and total obedience to the King. There is to be no hesitation or negotiation. You are to obey without debate or delay.

When you live by the principle of Matthew 6:33, then everything you do will relate to the priority of the Kingdom of God in your life. For example, your job becomes a ministry that allows you, by your conduct and work performance, to give visual testimony that attracts your coworkers to the Kingdom. It allows you a way in which you can glorify the King of the Kingdom. The Bible says, "Therefore, whether you eat or drink, or whatever you do, do all to the glory of God" (1 Corinthians 10:31). Likewise, when the Kingdom of God is first in your life, you will do nothing that detracts or interferes with that Kingdom. You will not have to wrestle with certain decisions, because your activities will be directed by and focused on whatever the King would have you do. When the Kingdom of God becomes your priority, then righteousness will become your practice, and the conduct of your life will be in accordance with the moral principles prescribed by the King in His Word. You will "not present your members as instruments of unrighteousness to sin, but (will) present yourselves to God as being alive from the dead and your members as instruments of righteousness to God" (Romans 6:13).

Jesus spoke the words of Matthew 6:33 after He talked about all the basic needs of life concerning which people spend so much of their time worrying and pursuing. Worry is a sure sign that we are not focusing on what we ought to, but God will not take second place in the list of our concerns. Essentially Jesus says that if we get the order correct and establish the right priority, the things about which we are worried will be "added" to us. He assures us that God knows our needs, even more clearly than we do, and He will supply those needs (see Philippians 4:19). The word translated "added" literally means "to lay beside," in the sense of giving more or increasing. In other words, as we give priority to the Kingdom of God, not striving after and worrying over the needs of life, we find along the way that God supplies what we need and even more.

The life of citizens of the Kingdom of God should be radically different from the rest of the world who do not know God. The contrast should be stark because their priorities are different from the world, their treasure is stored in heaven, and their focus is on serving and loving God. They are not citizens of the earth trying to get to heaven, but citizens of heaven making their way through this world. They belong to what the Bible calls "a holy nation" (1 Peter 2:9), the only Christian nation on earth, a nation within the nations.

Kingdom Allegiance

Proclamation is not necessarily participation. Being a part of God's Kingdom is not just declaring yourself a part of God's Kingdom; it is living as a citizen under King Jesus. If you do this, there is power in Him. This Kingdom is not just a theory or something to talk about; it is powerful and can change lives. "For the kingdom of God is not in word but in power" (1 Corinthians 4:20. Those who are part of the Kingdom just don't talk about the King; they obey and follow the King.

To be a citizen of any kingdom is to accept and obey its laws; therefore, to be a citizen of the Kingdom of God is to accept and obey the laws of God. The Kingdom of God is not a democracy or a republic. Nobody voted God in, and nobody can vote Him out. In fact, nobody has a vote at all. God is sovereign in the absolute sense of the word, and nobody can be within His Kingdom without total submission to His lordship. In ancient Rome the army required every soldier to take an oath of allegiance called the *sacramentum militare*. The oath was a test of unwavering loyalty to the emperor, in which the soldier swore to obey unquestionably any order of the emperor, administered through the general, never desert the army, and never seek to avoid death for the Roman state. Citizens of God's Kingdom can do no less.

Kingdom Standards

In the Kingdom of God, there is absolutely no legality, but there is the highest standard, as high as God Himself. There can be no higher standard than the one Jesus put before us in Matthew 5:48: "You shall be perfect, just as your Father in heaven is perfect." We can never be perfect in the sense that we never sin. "If we say that we have no sin, we deceive ourselves, and the truth is not in us" (1 John 1:8). God knows we sin, and He has made provision for us through Jesus' high priestly work (1 John 2:1). Jesus is telling us in Matthew 5:48 that God is the standard against which everything else is measured.

That statement is found in what we call the Sermon on the Mount, recorded in Matthew 5-7. I like to refer to this teaching of Jesus as The Kingdom Manifesto because here Jesus tells us what the Kingdom of God is all about, as far as a standard of living is concerned. The sermon covers all areas of life and tells us how we are to conduct ourselves as Kingdom citizens. Jesus outlines the primary attributes of people who receive the rule of the Kingdom. There are nine direct references to "the Kingdom" in this sermon, each calling for a particular character trait: humility (5:3); willingness to suffer persecution (5:10); complete obedience to God's commandments and teaching others to obey (5:19); refusal to substitute false piety for genuine righteousness (5:20); a life of prayer (6:10, 13); giving priority to spiritual over material values (6:33); and above all, acknowledging Christ's lordship by obeying the revealed will of God (7:21). To give an exposition of Matthew 5-7, even in a cursory manner, would be far beyond the scope of this volume. However, a forthcoming publication will be an exposition of the Sermon on the Mount entitled *The Kingdom Manifesto.*

At this point, I simply want to comment upon the one word that summarizes the moral demands of the Kingdom of God. That word is "holy." We have already seen that this is the word that God used to designate the nation He chose through which He would provide for the redemption of the world. In Exodus 11:7 we read that God wants us to "know that the Lord does make a difference between the Egyptians and Israel." The word holy means "set apart for a purpose," "separate," and "different." The Bible says that God is holy, meaning that He is the majestic, morally lofty one, separated from humanity, not only as a finite material creature but as a sinful, impure creature. He is in a category all to Himself. 1 Samuel 2:2 proclaims God as the ultimate model of holiness: "No one is holy like the Lord, for there is none besides You, nor is there any rock like our God."

God is different, and His Kingdom is certainly different, quite unlike any earthly kingdom, especially in its standards. It's a Kingdom that regards practically everything in our human world the opposite way. Enemies are to be blessed; wealth is to be given away; to live a full life we must live not for ourselves but for others; the last will be first; to find life you must lose life; to be strong you must be weak; selfless love must always come first; mercy triumphs over judgment; the old must go and the new must come; external actions or appearances or facades are not as important as the attitude of our hearts; a King who humbles Himself unto death, even death on a cross; death defeated by love. It's all completely upside down, and the citizens of this Kingdom are supposed to live this way.

And that explains why the people of the world will never understand the people of the Kingdom. Kingdom citizens have made a commitment to the lordship of Jesus Christ, and that commitment guides everything they do. They look at life in a different way, they make their decisions on a different basis, and they have an entirely different value system. That difference affects all areas of life, in business dealings, friendships, leisure activities, how to spend money, or how to vote in an election. This commitment to the King separates the people of the Kingdom from the people of the world, which is why Kingdom citizens are misunderstood and often ridiculed, scorned, and persecuted.

When applied to persons, the basic idea of holy is a relationship, that is, belonging to God to be used in His service or dedicated to Him. But it also means moral purity, becoming like the God to whom we belong. It's God's holiness that sets Him apart from everything else, and it's our holiness that sets us apart from and makes us distinctive from the world. Belonging to God, we cannot belong to the world. Being dedicated to Him, we cannot be devoted to anything else.

God saves us so that we may become holy. "As He who called you is holy, you also be holy in all your conduct, because it is written, 'Be holy, for I am holy'" (1 Peter 1:15-16). Ephesians 1:4 states that God chose us in Christ "that we should be holy and without blame before Him." Ephesians 5:27 tells us that Christ's purpose in cleansing the Church is "that He might present her to Himself a glorious church, not having spot or wrinkle or any such thing, but that she should be holy and without blemish." The purpose of God in saving us was not just to take us to heaven when we die. Heaven is a bonus, but the real purpose behind God's saving grace is for holiness, for life on this earth, that we might be transformed into the likeness of Jesus (see Romans 8:29).

To be holy means to be set apart for a purpose, and that purpose is to manifest God's character to the world. Having been bought with a price, we belong to God, and we are to glorify Him in our bodies (1 Corinthians 6:19-20). To glorify God means to reveal and demonstrate His character. In order to do that, we must be holy. Therefore, the standard by which Kingdom citizens are expected to live is God's own holy and perfect character. This standard is held up before us throughout the New Testament, and our holiness is patterned after Jesus Christ (1 Peter 1:15; Matthew 5:48; John 17:19; 2 Corinthians 7:1; 1 John 2:6). Before we can embrace this new standard of living, we must abandon the old lifestyle we knew in the world (1 Peter 1:14). The formative influence of our lives is no longer our desires, but the character of Jesus. Our conduct is to be shaped by His holiness. We are to walk in the light as He is in the light (1 John 1:6-7).

As we have noted, the motivation for all Kingdom conduct is "You shall be holy, for I am holy." Something is right or wrong not because of what we might think about it, but because of what God says about it. For example, even though psychologists, sociologists, Hollywood celebrities, politicians, and liberal bishops may declare that homosexuality is physically normal, mentally healthy, emotionally safe, and socially acceptable, that doesn't make it morally right. It is sin, simply because God says it is. The vote of anybody else on the subject is not necessary.

Regrettably, many contemporary convictions about what is right and what is wrong are being formed by public opinion rather than by God's holiness and God's Word. This statement is evidenced by the wholesale compromise of churches, denominations, and individuals on issues such as homosexuality, same-gender marriage, transgenderism, and abortion. People scream about human rights, but little is heard about divine rights. The fear of being labeled a narrow-minded bigot who wants to deny a person's rights influences a lot of people more than the holiness of God does. At one time the Church was a voice, not an echo, but it seems that we have forgotten that the Church is supposed to correct the spirit of the age, not catch it.

God's call for Kingdom citizens to be holy includes the power to become holy. What God demands He provides. With the call to Kingdom living and ministry comes the assurance that the Holy Spirit will produce in us His fruit, Christlike qualities of life, love, and a holy character (John 15:1-17; Galatians 5:22-23). The same Spirit distributes gifts of power for Kingdom service (1 Corinthians 12:7-11; Romans 12:3-8; Acts 1:8).

Kingdom living means for us commitment and cooperation. We are to be serious: "Gird up the loins of your mind" (1 Peter 1:13). We are to "be sober" (1 Peter 1:13). We are not to be intoxicated with the things of the world, but to keep morally alert. We are to be separated: "Not conforming yourselves to the former lusts" (1 Peter 1:14). There must be a definite and daily break with the ways of the world.

Kingdom Activity

Before Jesus ascended into heaven, He charged His followers to preach the gospel and make disciples around the world (Matthew 28:18-20; Mark 16:15; Luke 24:47-49; John 20:21; Acts 1:8). At the same time, He promised His presence and the enabling power of the Holy Spirit. That commission and that promise are still in effect "even to the end of the age." He also gave instructions concerning our responsibility to use faithfully whatever abilities God has bestowed upon us.

In a parable recorded in Luke 19:11-27, Jesus made it vividly clear that every individual Kingdom citizen is to be engaged in ministry activity until He returns. As he was approaching Jerusalem near the end of His ministry, He realized that many people expected Him to go into the city to take over the throne and become king. But it wasn't going to happen the way they expected. It's true that there was to be a Kingdom, but not a physical kingdom established by the force of arms. Instead, Jesus will suffer and die and rise again. Then He will leave for an indeterminate time, after which He will return as the rightful King. During the time between His departure and His return, we are His servants, and He has entrusted something to each of us. We are not supposed to sit around waiting for Him to return. Rather, we are to be actively doing business for Him. Our responsibility is to use what He has given us, and when He returns there will be an audit of what we have done.

The people who heard this parable readily understood it, because it was based on an actual historical event that had happened some years earlier. After the death of King Herod, his son Archelaus was given rulership over Judea, but he had to travel to Rome to be confirmed as king by the emperor. However, many people of Judea didn't want him to be king, so they sent a delegation to Rome to express their bitter opposition to his claim as king. Their attempt failed, and Archelaus returned successfully from Rome. When he returned, he ordered the execution of those who had opposed him.

In the parable a nobleman goes on an extended trip to be crowned king. Most of the people hate him and send a delegation to oppose his coronation. Before he leaves, he entrusts money to several of his servants to invest on his behalf. Two of them make investments that earn successful returns. A third servant is afraid to take the risk, so he puts the money in a safe place, and it earns no return. When the master returns as king, he rewards the two servants who made money by promoting them to high positions. He punishes the servant who kept the money safe but unproductive. Then he commands the execution of all who opposed him.

Kingdom citizens are to use faithfully and productively everything that the King has given us. That principle applies not only to money but to every gift entrusted to us (see Romans 12:6; 1 Corinthians 12:4-7; 1 Peter 4:10). When Jesus returns, He will judge what we have done. Those who are found faithful will be rewarded generously. The ones in this group are enthusiastic and diligent in their service. Those who are negligent will receive nothing. Citizens in this group are content to get by and do nothing more than lip service. Then there are those who openly reject Jesus. There is no neutrality. You are either for Jesus or against Him. He offers forgiveness for those who are opposed to Him, but there will be judgment if they spurn that opportunity.

God has given every one of us a gift, and He expects us to use the gift for His glory. That means that we are stewards and must work diligently and responsibly with what God has entrusted to us—our time, our talents, our minds, our money, and our strength. We must be faithful to do what He calls us to do with the resources He has given us to do it. We are to work steadily in the day-by-day business of the Kingdom of God, knowing that the King is coming back soon, and we want to be ready.

THE TRIUMPH OF THE KINGDOM

When Jesus stood on trial before Pilate, the Roman governor sought several times to release Him, because he considered Jesus to be no threat to Rome (John 18:31, 38; 19:4-12). He had no soldiers, and His own nation rejected Him. He even offered no defense to save His life. Pilate may have seen no threat in Jesus, but little did he know that the small group that followed Him would be victorious against the seemingly unconquerable might of the Roman emperor. It was His Kingdom that brought down the kingdom of Rome, as it will bring down all the kingdoms of Earth.

We have seen how the Old Testament repeatedly emphasizes the eternal nature of the Kingdom of God. When God established a covenant with David that through him there would be an everlasting Kingdom, He stressed that the covenant was unconditionally unalterable and that it depended on God's strength and faithfulness. God said to David: "When your days are fulfilled and you rest with your fathers, I will set up your seed after you, who will come from your body, and I will establish his kingdom. He shall build a house for My name, and I will establish the throne of his kingdom forever" (2 Samuel 7:12-13). We read later that the eternal nature of the Kingdom does not depend on David; it does not depend upon David's heirs; it does not depend on human ingenuity or strength or genius; it depends on God! "I have made a covenant with

My chosen. I have sworn to My servant David: 'Your seed I will establish forever and build up your throne to all generations'" (Psalm 89:3-4). God later adds: "My covenant I will not break, nor alter the word that has gone out of My lips. Once I have sworn by My holiness; I will not lie to David: His seed shall endure forever, and his throne as the sun before Me; it shall be established forever like the moon, even like the faithful witness in the sky" (Psalm 89:34-37).

God says that as long as the sun shines in the sky and as long as the moon shines by night, just so long will His covenant be unconditionally unalterable before David. The prophet Jeremiah records the same vow: "Thus says the Lord: 'If you can break My covenant with the day and My covenant with the night, so that there will not be day and night in their season, then My covenant may also be broken with David My servant, so that he shall not have a son to reign on his throne'" (Jeremiah 33:20-21). As though that were not enough, God repeats that same unconditional covenant. Swearing by Himself, by His holiness, He says: "If my covenant is not with day and night, and if I have not appointed the ordinances of heaven and earth, then I will cast away the descendants of Jacob and David My servant, so that I will not take any of his descendants to be rulers" (Jeremiah 33:25-26). God repeatedly gives His word to David: "Your house and your kingdom shall be established forever before you. Your throne shall be established forever" (Psalm 89:16).

Daniel, to whom Jesus referred as a prophet (Matthew 24:15), wrote: "And in the days of these kings the God of heaven will set up a kingdom which shall never be destroyed; and the kingdom shall not be left to other people; it shall break in pieces and consume all these kingdoms, and it shall stand forever. Inasmuch as you saw that the stone was cut out of the mountain without hands, and that it broke in pieces the iron, the bronze, the clay, the silver, and the gold—the great God has made known to the king what will come to pass" (Daniel 2:44-45). He also recorded this vision: "I was watching in the night visions, and behold, One like the Son of Man, coming with the clouds of heaven! He came to the Ancient of Days, and they brought Him near before Him. Then to Him was given dominion and glory and a kingdom, that all peoples, nations, and languages should serve Him. His dominion is an everlasting dominion, which shall not pass away, and His kingdom the one which shall not be destroyed" (Daniel 7:13-14).

The world is full of nations with rulers, kings, and presidents. Many of them are very powerful, but all the kingdoms of this world are imperfect and at times corrupt. History and experience tell us that they cannot last. There is but one Kingdom that is eternal, perfect, flawless, and incorruptible. It is God's Kingdom, and it will last forever. When the angel Gabriel came to Mary, he announced that she would give birth to a Son who "will reign over the house of Jacob forever, and of His kingdom there will be no end" (Luke 1:33).

Hebrews 12:28 says that we have received "a kingdom which cannot be shaken." History has shown us the collapse of the great kingdoms of this world. There has been the establishment of no earthly kingdom that cannot be shaken and removed. Mankind's ultimate fallacy is to refuse the Kingdom of God and set up their own kingdoms, which they think are going to be durable and everlasting. And they have built kingdoms in many ways, but all of them come and go.

The most common have been great military kingdoms, which dominated until a stronger power arose. The earliest and mightiest of the ancient empires was Egypt, but only archaeological relics remain to testify to its greatness. The Assyrians were the scourge of civilization for 200 years, beginning in the ninth century B.C. Then the Babylonians, with unparalleled wealth and military strength, dominated for the next two centuries. But an even stronger power, Persia, came along. This kingdom seemed to be so invincible that it would last forever. It was the first kingdom to cover multiple world regions, dominating 45 million people on portions of three continents.

Then the kingdom of Greece arose, led by a young military genius called Alexander. He conquered in just a few years more territory than anyone else before him, which included all the known civilized world. It was an amazing kingdom, great in every respect, and it appeared to be indestructible. However, the kingdom dissolved only a few years after Alexander's death. By the way, history has dubbed him with the epithet "the Great," but in the book of Daniel, he is pictured as a goat (see Daniel 8).

Another kingdom came up on the stage of world history, the Roman Empire, one of the most astonishing phenomena the world has ever seen. Rome conquered the entire civilized world, not only in a military sense but in every other way. Finally, here was a kingdom that would last forever. Even its capital city Rome was called "the Eternal City." However, after a few centuries, hordes of tribes from northern Europe conquered and ended the undefeatable Roman Empire.

It's the same story with all great empires—China, the Caliphate, the Mongol, the Ottoman, Spain, Russia, and others. Kingdoms after kingdoms have emerged with the proclamation of everlasting existence, only to vanish. What about more recent times? A man named Adolf Hitler boasted that he had built a Reich that would last a thousand years. It lasted twelve years. Many people would argue that the greatest empire in history was the British Empire. The boast was that the sun never set on the British Empire. Indeed, it was the largest empire in history, and at its peak in 1922, it stretched across one-fourth of the land surface of the earth and embraced one-fourth of the world's population. It was thought to be unshakable and durable, but it collapsed. The man who believed in it the most, the man who said that he had not become the prime minister to preside over the liquidation of the British Empire, witnessed its dissolution. That man was Winston Churchill.

The United States is rushing blindly down the same path, led by politicians who either know nothing of the laws of the Kingdom of God or choose to ignore them. The way things are now, the shriek of the American eagle is nothing more than the feeble peep of a canary.

All kingdoms that men build are shakable and will collapse, and that includes not only kingdoms built on military might but all kinds of kingdoms. For example, there is the kingdom of philosophy and reason, in which earthly wisdom is exalted and the Bible is dismissed as a collection of fairy tales preying on the emotionalism of vulnerable people. There is the kingdom of science, which not only relies on scientific facts but accepts unprovable theories as reality. It's interesting that many things called laws, certainties, and absolutes in past years, such as the indivisibility of the atom, are now shown to be false. Financial, political, sports, entertainment, and all other man-made empires will be shaken. Everything that is part of the world system will be removed in the final shaking of God. Even the whole world as we know it will be convulsed in a final cataclysm, and nothing will remain (See Isaiah 13:13; 24:18-20; 2 Peter 3:10; Revelation 6:12-17; 16:17-19). But there is one Kingdom that cannot be moved. The glorious Kingdom of God is an everlasting Kingdom.

All of us right now are in one kingdom or another. Those who are not in the Kingdom of God are in a kingdom opposed to the sovereignty of God. There are warnings throughout the Bible about the consequences of refusing to enter the Kingdom of God. In the context of what is written concerning the shaking of the earth, there is an appeal to listen to "Him who speaks from heaven" (Hebrews 12:25). Everywhere in the Bible there is the free offer to enter the everlasting glory and eternal joy and happiness of the Kingdom of God. We have discussed the way to enter in the section entitled "Entering the Kingdom." The way is simple. Repent. Acknowledge your sin, your failure, your inability to save yourself by your own righteousness. Believe the gospel. Believe that Jesus is the Lord and Savior who came to die for you to save you and to offer you free pardon and forgiveness, a new life, the peace, righteousness, and joy of His kingdom, and eternal life. "Believe on the Lord Jesus Christ, and you will be saved" (Acts 16:31). You can live for this world, or you can live for the Kingdom of God. The choice is yours.

CONCLUSION

What we call "history" is really "His story," the record of God's dealings with humanity. The Bible teaches that the universe, including the earth, had a definite beginning at a definite point in time. It also teaches that man is not the result of some quirky evolutionary process. According to the Bible, God created the earth and its inhabitants with a purpose, and history is the story of the unfolding of God's purpose on the earth. Having created the heavens and the earth, God gave Adam and Eve dominion over the whole planet as His stewards. But when they disobeyed, they forfeited their authority as stewards into the hands of Satan. From that day the whole world has been the domain of Satan. It is still God's world by creation, but Satan has usurped man's rightful authority and set himself up as the ruler of a counter-kingdom to the reign of God.

However, God sought to restore what man had lost through his rebellion. He would do it by raising up a nation through which He would bless the world with redemption. He chose one man, Abraham, as the father of that nation and promised that out of his descendants, a deliverer would arise to reign victoriously over an everlasting Kingdom. That deliverer was God Himself, entering the human race in the person of His Son, the Lord Jesus Christ. God sent this message over the centuries through prophets, priests, kings, and poets. He gave Abraham the privilege of seeing a glimpse of the glory of that Kingdom. Moses saw it from afar. David learned about it directly from God and wrote extensively about the King and the Kingdom. The Old Testament prophets spoke again and again of a coming Kingdom on the earth. They foresaw a time when God's Messiah would rule the world from David's throne in Jerusalem, and they wrote graphic and detailed descriptions of the Kingdom.

Finally, "when the fullness of the time had come," that is, when in God's timetable everything was in place, "God sent forth His Son" (Galatians 4:4). The New Testament unmistakably proclaims that the Lord Jesus Christ is the promised Messiah. With the arrival of the King came the Kingdom, but when Jesus was crucified, it appeared that Satan had won a decisive victory. Then Jesus rose from the dead, as He said He would, and it became clear that He was the victor in the conflict to reclaim dominion over the earth. But the Kingdom of God will not be ultimately established until Jesus the King returns triumphantly to Earth. That is where history is headed. That's the goal toward which the movements of history are pointed. The Kingdom of God is what history is all about. All the strands of history will converge in the return of the Lord. God "purposed in Himself that in the dispensation of the fullness of the times He might gather together in one all things in Christ, both which are in heaven and which are on earth, in Him" (Ephesians 2:10). That will be the last chapter in a story that began in the Garden of Eden.

And *that* is where history is going. The Kingdom of God is the goal toward which everything else is moving. It's the last chapter in a story that started in the Garden of Eden.

II
THE KING

WHO IS THE KING?

We have seen the purpose of God to establish His Kingdom on earth. When God made man, He gave him dominion over all His handiwork. Adam forfeited to Satan the authority that God had given to him, but God's purpose concerning the Kingdom did not waiver or change. Consequently, when we look at the Bible, from its beginning to its ending, we find outlined and revealed the purpose of God to build a Kingdom. And God never deviates from what He has revealed in His Word. We have traced the concept of the Kingdom through the centuries. We have discussed the necessary passports for entry into the Kingdom, and we have seen the things that are hindrances and barriers that make entry into the Kingdom difficult or even impossible.

You cannot have a kingdom without a king, so who is the King? Answer that question correctly and live by what you answer, and everything else will be right. Answer it incorrectly and everything else will be wrong. Jesus is the King of the Kingdom, so we turn our eyes to Him. But before we do so, we must keep in mind that all we could ever say or write concerning Him could never tell the whole story of who Jesus is and what He has done. When the apostle John came to the end of his story about Jesus, He said, "And there are also many other things that Jesus did, which if they were written one by one, I suppose that even the world itself could not contain the books that would be written." The Bible speaks of "the unsearchable riches of Christ" (Ephesians 3:8). There is a popular poem about the life of Jesus Christ, the author of which is frequently cited as unknown, but probably was written by James Allen Francis.

He was born in an obscure village, the child of a peasant. He grew up in another village, where he worked in a carpenter shop until he was 30. Then, for three years, he was an itinerant preacher.

He never wrote a book. He never held an office. He never had a family or owned a home. He didn't go to college. He never lived in a big city. He never traveled 200 miles from the place where he was born. He did none of the things that usually accompany greatness. He had no credentials but himself.

He was only 33 when the tide of public opinion turned against him. His friends ran away. One of them denied him. He was turned over to his enemies and went through the mockery of a trial. He was nailed to a cross between two thieves. While he was dying, his executioners gambled for his garments, the only property he had on earth. When he was dead, he was laid in a borrowed grave, through the pity of a friend.

Twenty centuries have come and gone, and today he is the central figure of the human race. I am well within the mark when I say that all the armies that ever marched, all the navies that ever sailed, all the parliaments that ever sat, all the kings that ever reigned--put together--have not affected the life of man on this earth as much as that one, solitary life.

I want to expand the words of Mr. Francis by adding some reflections on the life of Jesus. the birth of Jesus divided history into B.C. and A.D. Although He wrote no books, more books have been written about Him than any other person who ever lived. He never painted a picture, composed music, or wrote poetry, and yet He has been the inspiration of the greatest art, music, and poetry that the world has ever known. He never raised an army, yet billions have surrendered to Him, and millions have been martyred in serving Him. He never traveled extensively, yet He is known intimately around the globe. He never spoke to more than a few thousand people at one time, yet today one-third of the population of the world claim allegiance to Him. He never had an advanced education, yet more schools, colleges, universities, and seminaries have been established in His name than any other person who ever lived. He never owned any property, and whereas "foxes have holes and birds of the air have nests," He had "nowhere to lay His head." He was relatively unknown outside the circle of His friends and countrymen, yet today He is acclaimed and worshiped as the King of kings.

In the year 1935, the noted historian H. G. Wells compiled a list of what he called the ten greatest men of history. Even though he was not a Christian, he named Jesus as number one on the list. However, Jesus doesn't belong on that list, because no mortal man can compare with Him. There has never been another one like Him. As we have seen, the Kingdom of God is unlike any other kingdom, and the King is unlike any other king. It is His uniqueness that makes our faith different. You can take Buddha out of Buddhism and still have Buddhism. You can take Mohammed out of Islam and still have Islam. You can take Confucius out of Confucianism and still have Confucianism. But you cannot take Jesus Christ out of Christianity and still have Christianity. Buddha, Mohammed, Confucius, and others left their teachings, and their followers try to live by those teachings. The teachers themselves are not necessary. But Christianity is not a code; it is not a creed; it is not a code; it is not a church; it is Christ and a vital living relationship with Him. To take Him out of Christianity is like taking the notes out of music or numbers out of mathematics. There is nothing left. The founders of the ethnic religions of the world taught and said, "Here is the way," but Jesus said, "I am the way." They taught and said, "Here is a philosophy that points to the truth," but Jesus said, "I am the truth." They taught and said, "Here is the pathway to life. Follow that." But Jesus said, "I am the life."

Jesus Is God

The title Kingdom of God means that it is a Kingdom in which God is King. Therefore, to say that Jesus is King is to acknowledge the deity of Jesus, a belief essential to our faith. Every citizen of the Kingdom of God looks at Jesus and makes the same confession as Thomas— "My Lord and my God!" (John 20:28).

The Claims of the Disciples

Throughout the New Testament, the followers of Jesus referred to Him as "Lord," which is to say that Jesus is God. The Hebrew Old Testament was translated into Greek about 200 years before Jesus was born. It was translated in order that Greek-speaking Jews who lived in lands beyond Palestine would be able to have the Scriptures in their own language. This Greek Old Testament is called the Septuagint. When they were translating the Old Testament and came to the word Yahweh, Jehovah, the translators wondered how they could translate it into Greek. This was the sacred Hebrew name for God, and there was no way they could transliterate it into Greek. They finally decided they would translate the name Yahweh by the Greek word *ho kurios*, the Lord. That's why you will find many times in the English versions of the Old Testament the word LORD, all in capital letters, you know that it's a translation of Yahweh. The first followers of Jesus understood that when they called Jesus *ho kurios*, they were actually calling Him God.

They went further than that. They not only called Jesus Jehovah, but they boldly applied to Jesus verses in the Old Testament used in reference to Jehovah. I will give one example and list several others. In Isaiah 45:23, Jehovah God swore by Himself that every knee shall bow to Him, and every tongue shall swear by His name. In Philippians 2:10-11, the apostle Paul dared to apply that verse to Jesus: "Therefore God also has highly exalted Him and given Him the name which is above every name, that at the name of Jesus" (not at the name of Jehovah), "every knee should bow . . . and every tongue should confess that Jesus Christ is Lord." Check also these comparisons: Isaiah 44:6 with Revelation 1:17; Isaiah 43:11 with Titus 2:13; Psalm 24:10 with 1 Corinthians 2:8. It's clear that the apostles applied to Jesus not only the title of Jehovah, but also verses in the Old Testament that applied to Jehovah. The fact that they transferred to Jesus these titles and verses has only one meaning. They were convinced that Jesus Christ was God, and they worshiped Him as they worshiped Jehovah.

Hebrews 1:3 asserts that Jesus is the brightness of God's glory and the express image of God's person. He does not bring God's glory. He is that glory. He does not reveal God's glory. He is the glory of God. Jesus is "the light of the world" (John 8:12), and He came to give light to everyone (John 1:9). His glorified countenance is "like the sun shining in its strength" (Revelation 1:16). In His face is "the light of the knowledge of the glory of God" (2 Corinthians 4:6). "The express image" has the idea of something that is made with a dye or a mold. When you take the mold away, you will see that the thing that was stamped is identical to the thing that stamped it.

The Claims of Jesus

Jesus was barely 30 years of age when He began His ministry. He was from a very humble family in an obscure village. He was a carpenter with calloused hands. He had no money, no recognition, no credentials, and no influence. But He began making such extravagant claims for Himself that even His friends and family questioned His sanity (Mark 3:21; John 7:5). Practically everything Jesus said was a claim to divinity, either direct or indirect. In His first public preaching, He announced that the long-expected Kingdom of God is going to be inaugurated by Him and that He is going to occupy the chief place in it. He even calls God's Kingdom "My Kingdom" (John 18:36). In the synagogue of Nazareth, where He was brought up, He read a passage from the prophecy of Isaiah and had the effrontery to say that it referred to Himself (Luke 4:16-21). In fact, He asserted that all the sacred Scriptures witnessed to Him and that He is their fulfillment (Matthew 5:17).

He referred to God as His Father, something no pious Jew would do. Even when He taught His disciples to address God as Father, He made it clear that His relationship to God as Father was different from theirs (see John 20:17). He explained His healing of a blind man on the Sabbath by saying, "My Father has been working until now, and I have been working." Immediately "the Jews sought all the more to kill Him because He not only broke the Sabbath, but also said that God was His Father, making Himself equal with God" (John 5:17-18). Later, after referring to God as His Father in His teaching, "the Jews took up stones again to stone Him," with the explanation that they were stoning Him for blasphemy, pretending that He was God (John 10:31-33).

Jesus equated one's attitude to Himself with one's attitude to God. He said that to know Him was to know God (John 8:19; 14:7); to see Him was to see God (John 12:45; 14:9); to believe in Him was to believe in God (John 12:44; 14:1); to receive Him was to receive God (Mark 9:37); to hate Him was to hate God (John 15:23); and to honor Him was to honor God (John 5:23).

As we shall see, Jesus took it for granted that He was entitled to the worship that was due to God alone. He assumed the right to forgive sins, a prerogative belonging only to God (John 8:1-11; Mark 2:5-11).

Jesus continuously preached Himself. He spoke of Himself as the Son of Man 44 times. He called God His Father in an exclusive sense 24 times. He affirmed His unique and exclusive relationship to God 10 times. Twenty-five times He pointed to His death as divinely ordained or having redemptive significance. He announced beforehand His resurrection from the dead 17 times. He promised to be spiritually present while physically absent from His disciples three times. Seventeen times He pointed to Himself as the supreme motive of life, calling people to act and to suffer in His name and for His sake. He claimed supreme moral and religious authority 33 times. He claimed to be the final judge who would determine the everlasting destiny of people 12 times. He claimed or exercised authority over nature and manifested supernatural knowledge 43 times. He accepted the title Son of God nine times. He claimed the title Son of God three times. Five times He affirmed that He held a unique position as the Lord and Master of people. Forty-four times He claimed to be the one in whom the ultimate purpose of God was fulfilled. "I am the way, the truth, and the life." "I am the light of the world." "I am the bread of life." "I am the true vine." "I am the good shepherd." "If anyone is thirsty, let Him come to Me and drink." He promised that prayer offered in His name will be answered (John 14:13-14). He claimed to be the Lord of the realm of death (John 2:19; 5:25-29; 11:25-26).

As we shall see, He declared His pre-existence many times. He said that love of Him was proof that one was a child of God (John 8:42). He declared in Matthew 28:18 that He had universal power. At His trial Jesus said, "You will see the Son of Man sitting at the right hand of the Power and coming on the clouds of heaven" (Matthew 26:64). It's no wonder that the high priest thought he had an open and shut case when he heard those words. He exclaimed, "What further need do we have of witnesses? Look, now you have heard His blasphemy" (Matthew 26:65). Jesus not only made claims for Himself, but He placed claims upon people. In Matthew 10:37 He declared that a person's relation to Him must take precedence over every other relation; that people must give themselves to Him without reserve; that no rival claims, however strong, no natural affection, however legitimate and sacred, must stand in the way of His claim upon us.

Jesus made many other claims and gave many other promises that speak of divine authority. One of His clearest claims to deity, and the most infuriating to the Jewish religious leaders, is found in John 8:56-59. The Jews were always boasting that they were children of Abraham. When Jesus said, "Abraham rejoiced to see My day," they responded that since He was not even 50 years old, it was impossible for Him to have seen Abraham. Jesus replied with an emphatic assertion: "Most assuredly, I say to you, before Abraham was, I AM." They understood exactly what He was saying and attempted to stone Him. Why were they infuriated? The clear answer is found in Exodus 3:14. God had called Moses to lead the Hebrews out of Egyptian captivity. When Moses asked God what he should tell the people when they asked who sent him, God replied: "I AM WHO I AM . . . Thus you shall say to the children of Israel, I AM has sent me to you."

This was the most sacred name for Jehovah in all the Bible. God said "I AM," not "I WAS," or "I WILL BE." He is the great eternal self-existent God who never had a beginning and never will have an ending. By applying this term to Himself, Jesus was claiming to be God. It's no wonder that they sought to kill Him, because they considered Him to be guilty of the most abject blasphemy possible.

What can you make of all those claims of Jesus, and many more that we have not mentioned? You can say that He was a self-centered imposter, a fraud, a deceiver, a liar, or that He had a fixed delusion about Himself. Or you can say that He was true. Those are the only alternatives unless you add the possibility that He was a lunatic. When we consider the evidence of the life and teachings of Jesus and the witness of others, both contemporary to Him and throughout history, it would be very difficult to maintain that He was a liar or an imposter. For me the decision is easy. I believe in Jesus for reasons that are historical, biblical, and personal. Jesus is a fact of history, and He is the turning point of history.

The Bible is the story of redemption through the Lord Jesus Christ, and I believe the Bible is true. The wonder of fulfilled prophecies in the Bible, the unity of the Bible, the accuracy of the Bible, and the longevity of the Bible are convincing and logical arguments that the Bible is indeed the Word of God. But primarily, I believe in Jesus because the Holy Spirit enabled me to believe, and through faith I had a personal encounter with the Lord Jesus Christ and entered a living relationship with Him.

His Divine Attributes

The descriptions of Jesus Himself in the New Testament, as well as His activities and the worship He receives testify to His deity.

He Is Pre-existent

"In the beginning was the Word, and the Word was with God, and the Word was God" (John 1:1). The use of the word "beginning" in this statement does not denote a start but a state. It speaks of the pre-existence of Jesus. He always has been God, and He always will be God. The story of the life of Jesus does not begin in Bethlehem or Nazareth but in eternity. There never was a time when Jesus was not. He was not a created being. As we shall see later, He was born of the flesh, but before he was ever born of the flesh, He existed eternally with God the Father. Clearly taught in the New Testament is the fact that Jesus, the eternal, pre-existing Son of God, became man in order to reveal the Father and bring eternal life through His death and resurrection. John 20:30-31 explicitly states His purpose: "Jesus did many other signs in the presence of His disciples, which are not written in this book; but these are written that you may believe that Jesus is the Christ, the Son of God, and that believing you may have life in His name." Jesus repeatedly spoke of having been sent into the world by the Father, indicating that He had been with the Father (see Matthew 10:40; Mark 9:37; Luke 9:48; 10:16; John 5:23-24, 30, 37; 6:39; 7:16, 18, 28, 33; 8:16, 26-29; 9:4; 12:45, 49; 13:20; 14:25; 15:21; 16:5). The apostle Paul spoke of God sending Jesus into the world (Romans 8:3; Galatians 4:4). Paul also said that Jesus existed before all creation. Jesus Himself claimed to be pre-existent (John 3:13; 6:62; 8:58; 17:5).

The Bible teaches that before He came into this world, Jesus pre-existed in "the form of God" (Philippians 2:6). The word translated "form" does not refer to an external shape or likeness. It signifies one's inner, essential nature. The word also means something that cannot be given up or changed. In other words, this statement means that Jesus possesses the very nature of deity—prior to His birth in Bethlehem and following it. He always was, is, and forever shall be God. During the time that He lived on this earth as a man, He did not give up His deity. Some versions of the Bible translate Philippians 2:7 as He "emptied" Himself. He did not empty Himself of His divine nature, but He did lay aside the glories of heaven and the prerogatives of deity when He came to earth. 2 Corinthians 8:9 tells us "that though He was rich, yet for your sakes He became poor, that you through His poverty might become rich."

He Is the Word of God

We have already referred to John 1:1 in reference to the pre-existence of Jesus, but that verse tells us something else about Him. He is the Word of God, equal with and fully identical with God, divine in all respects. Essentially, however, "Word" means that Jesus reveals God to us. God speaks to us in Jesus in a language we can understand. Hebrews 1:1-2 provides a commentary on God's revelation in Jesus: "God, who at various times and in various ways spoke in time past to the fathers by the prophets, has in these last days spoken to us by His Son." This statement at the very beginning of the book of Hebrews is not an argument. It is an incredible announcement that Jesus Christ is God's last word to humanity. Up to the time that Jesus was born, God had been speaking to human beings gradually. He had spoken through nature. He had spoken through conscience. He had spoken through history. He had spoken through the Law. He had spoken through the prophets. But now in these last days, God has spoken in His Son. As we shall discover in our study of preparation for the King, it seems that Jesus was standing in the wings of history, and His shadow was cast centuries before He came. All the books of the Old Testament seem to flow like tributaries into a mighty river, and they all merge into the last word of God to humanity, who is Jesus Christ. All the shadows of the Old Testament find their substance in Jesus. All the voices of all the prophets blend as one to glorify the coming King. God spoke in various ways, but "when the fullness of the time" came (Galatians 4:4), God decreed that all He had to say to this world is Jesus Christ. Jesus is God's Word in fullness, in focus, and in finality. When you have said Jesus, you have said it all.

Why is Jesus called the Word, the *Logos*? The simple answer is that a word is an expression of an idea. Jesus is the expression of God. He articulates God. When you hear Jesus, you hear God. God knew that we could never comprehend Him, so He spoke to us in a language we can understand, and that is Jesus. In the book of Revelation, Jesus refers to Himself as the "Alpha and Omega" (Revelation 1:8; 21:6; 22:13; see 1:17-18; 2:8; 4:8). In the Greek alphabet, alpha is the first letter and omega is the last letter. If Jesus had been speaking to an English audience, He would say, "I am the A and Z." If you want to say anything in print, you use the alphabet, which is 26 letters in English. Everything in the English Bible is made up of just 26 letters. Jesus is saying that the same thing that is true about the written word is true about the living Word. Everything that God wants to say about Himself, He says in Jesus.

The Jewish rabbis used the first and the last letters of the Hebrew alphabet to denote the whole of anything, from beginning to end. Jesus as the beginning and end of all things is a reference that can apply only to the true God, who was at the beginning of all things and will be at the close. It's the same as saying that He has always existed and always will exist. The phrase is one of those used for Jehovah in the Old Testament and applied to Jesus in the New Testament. In other words, it identifies Jesus as God. In Isaiah 41:4, God says about Himself, "I am the first, and with the last I am He." In Isaiah 44:6, He says, "I am the First and I am the Last; besides Me there is no God." In Isaiah 48:12, God says, "I am He, I am the First, I am also the Last." Jesus is the Alpha and Omega, the first and the last, the beginning and the end.

He Is Creator

Jesus does those things that God alone can do and everything that God does, Jesus does. For example, Jesus is the *reason* of creation. The Bible declares, "All things were made through Him, and without Him nothing was made that was made" (John 1:3). All things, one by one, came into being through Jesus Christ. This assertion is first stated positively from the viewpoint of the past, and then it is stated negatively from the viewpoint of the present. Apart from Him not a single thing that exists came into being. Colossians 1:16 asserts that all things were created in Christ, through Christ, and for Christ, that is, Jesus is the sphere, agent, and aim of creation. He is the cause, head, and goal of creation. This verse even divides creation into categories—things animate and inanimate, visible and invisible, material and spiritual, human and super-human, rational and non-rational, heavenly and earthly, temporary and abiding, and anything else that can be conceived. Everything in the universe is traced to Christ as Creator and Sovereign. All things without exception, whether in the heavens above or on the earth beneath, owe their existence to Christ and look for their purpose in Him.

Yet the Bible says, "In the beginning, God created the heavens and the earth" (Genesis 1:1). Then who created the heavens and the earth, Jesus or God? The answer to that question is "yes." We are told that God has appointed His Son "heir of all things, through whom also He made the worlds" (Hebrews 1:2). That means that all things were made by Him and for Him.

Jesus is the *ruler* of creation. Hebrews 1:3 says that He "upholds all things by the word of His power." The word uphold means to carry a load. Jesus keeps the universe running like a timepiece. He regulates the sun, the moon, and the stars. He holds the planets in their orbits. He keeps the cosmos from becoming chaos. Colossians 1:17 says that "in Him all things consist," which means they hang together. Jesus is the glue of the galaxies. Only as we ponder the relation of Christ's creation can we truly understand its significance, including our own creation. We can know little of creation until we know it as it stands related to Jesus. Single notes of music, thrown together without any regard to the principles of harmony, produce only nonsensical jingle-jangle. Separate Christ from creation, and there is no significance to creation.

Jesus is the *redeemer* of creation. Look again at Hebrews 1:3, speaking of Jesus: "When He had by Himself purged our sins, sat down at the right hand of the Majesty on high." The world as we know it is indescribably corrupt, ravaged by war, hatred, murder, greed, immorality, animalistic behavior, anarchy, and filth—everything that separates from the Kingdom of God. The world has a different view of this condition. The sociologist says it's a cultural lag. The psychologist calls it an emotional disorder. The philosopher calls it irrational thinking. The humanist calls it human weakness. The Marxist describes it as a class struggle. The criminologist calls it antisocial behavior. The Bible calls it sin. The reason the world cannot find the cure for its own sickness is that it never makes the right diagnosis and therefore always has the wrong prescription. The problem is sin, and Jesus is the Savior from sin. Hebrews 1:3 declares that Jesus purged our sins and that He did it by Himself. Nobody helped Him do it and nobody else can do it, "nor is there salvation in any other, for there is no other name under heaven given among men by which we must be saved" (Acts 4:12). Jesus took our sins, carried them to the cross, suffered, bled and died. Just before His last breath, He said, "It is finished," the translation of a word that literally means "paid in full." Then He sat down with God. His first recorded words in the Bible are, "I must be about My Father's business." The last recorded words of His earthly ministry are, "It is finished." He did what He came to do.

He Is Unique

There was never another man like the Lord Jesus, nor could there ever be, because, as we shall see He was God-man. When you read the Gospels, you will never find that Jesus never withdrew or modified any statement that He had made. Many things open by mistake, but none as frequently as the mouth, but Jesus never apologized for or altered or recanted anything He said. Never once did He apologize for anything He ever did. He never once sought advice from anybody. On one occasion He asked Phillip where they could buy bread to feed the multitudes. But the Bible makes it clear that He was testing Phillip, not asking for advice. He already knew what He was going to do (John 6:5-6). Jesus walked among doctors of the law and teachers, but instead of seeking to learn from them, He taught them and corrected them.

Jesus never justified any of His actions. Many things that He did were inexplicable and perplexed His followers, such as staying away when Lazarus was dying and sleeping during a storm. He saw no need to justify or apologize for anything He did. He just did it. He never asked anybody to pray for Him. In the Garden of Gethsemane, when He experienced an agonizing trial, He did tell the disciples to pray. But the prayer was not for Himself, but for them, lest they enter temptation.

Jesus never had to confess any wrongdoing and repent, because He had no sin for which to repent. Jesus was tempted, but the Bible affirms that He was completely sinless throughout His life on earth. The Bible says that God "made Him who knew no sin to be sin for us, that we might become the righteousness of God in Him" (2 Corinthians 5:21). The author of Hebrews described Jesus as the kind of high priest we need: "holy, harmless, undefiled, separate from sinners, and has become higher than the heavens" (Hebrews 7:6). And Peter said that Jesus "did not commit sin, and no deceit was found in his mouth." The Bible makes it clear that Jesus, though tempted in every way just as we are (Hebrews 4:15), never committed a sin (2 Corinthians 5:21; 1 John 3:5). The apostle Peter stated it plainly: "Who committed no sin, nor was deceit found in His mouth" (1 Peter 2:22).

He Is Worshipped

The followers of Jesus knew that only God was to be worshipped. Jesus Himself was acknowledging the first commandment when He said to Satan, "Get behind me, Satan! For it is written, 'You shall worship the Lord your God, and Him only you shall serve.'" On the island of Patmos, a glorious angel revealed some wonderful things to the apostle John. John was so impressed that he fell before the feet of the angel to worship him. The angel remonstrated John by saying, "See that you do not do that. For I am your fellow servant, and of your brethren the prophets, and of those who keep the words of this book. Worship God" (Revelation 22:8-9).

The worship of Jesus on earth began at his birth, with the shepherds (Luke 2:8-20) and later with the wise men (Matthew 2:11). The Gospels record other specific instances of worship, such as that offered by a blind man to whom Jesus gave sight (John 9:38), the women who saw the risen Lord (Matthew 28:9), and the disciples (Matthew 28:17; Luke 24:52). Thomas was so overcome at the sight of the risen Jesus that he worshipped Him, crying out, "My Lord and my God!" (John 20:15). Keep in mind that both Jesus and an angel, in accordance with the first commandment, said that only God was to be worshipped. But on each occasion that devotees knelt at His feet to worship Him, Jesus accepted their worship instead of rebuking them. The point is that Jesus received due to Him worship meant only for God.

Jesus deserves our worship simply because He is God. In showing the superiority of Jesus over angels in Hebrews 1:4-13, the author says that Jesus "has by inheritance obtained a more excellent name than they" (v. 4). The "name" of Jesus is more than just a personal label. It refers to His person and position as divine. Having been born by conception of the Holy Spirit and not an earthly father, He "inherited" the name the *Son of God* from the heavenly Father (see Luke 1:30-35). None of the angels can claim to be God or born an earthly birth by a conception of the Holy Spirit. The role of Jesus as Creator and His work in reconciling God and man make Him "more excellent" than any other conceivable spiritual being. The following verses give explicit Old Testament proof that the Messiah, Jesus Christ, is not merely some angelic being. Rather, He is the unique and all-powerful Son of God. The angels worship Him, and if Jesus is not God, then heaven is filled with idolatrous angels.

Hebrews 1:8 emphatically proclaims the sovereign nobility of Jesus as King of the Kingdom of God: "To the Son He says: 'Your throne O God, is forever and ever; a scepter of righteousness is the scepter of Your kingdom.'" Jesus is King. He was born a King. We didn't vote Him in and we're not going to vote Him out. His Kingdom is forever.

PREPARING FOR THE KING

The Old Testament

We have considered many references in the Old Testament concerning the coming of the King of the Kingdom. Now, we must show how those pronouncements apply specifically to Jesus Christ, for He is the fulfillment of them all. It is a mistake to treat Jesus as an isolated phenomenon, disregarding His background in the Old Testament. Our King can rightly be understood only in the light of a purpose that reached back through prophets and patriarchs to the creation of the world, and that would reach forward to the consummation of which the prophets of old had spoken. In Acts 26:22-23, the apostle Paul claimed that when he preached about Jesus and the salvation He brought, he was "saying no other things than those which the prophets and Moses said would come—that the Christ would suffer, that He would be the first to rise from the dead and would proclaim light to the Jewish people and to the Gentiles." More particularly, he wrote that it was "according to the Scriptures" that Christ died and rose again (1 Corinthians 15:3-4).

Prophecies

From Genesis to Malachi the Old Testament presents a prophetic portrait of the Messiah King. The New Testament constantly refers to those prophecies. Acts 10:43 says, "To Him give all the prophets witness." The word "Him" refers to Jesus, and the phrase "the prophets" refers to the Old Testament. Jesus said in John 5:39 that the Scriptures testified concerning Him. Scripture at that time was exclusively what we know as the Old Testament. Christ was telling the Jews that had they known their Bibles, they would know that He was the promised King Messiah. When He emphasized what the Old Testament said about Him, His purpose was not to put undue emphasis on Himself, but to show how the prophecies were being fulfilled before their eyes.

Conservatively speaking, there are more than 400 Old Testament prophecies referring to the coming of Christ. Prophets told of Him "since the world began" (Luke 1:70). Some of the prophecies were remarkably specific concerning details that would take place in His life. There are nearly 50 prophecies of this sort, stating facts such as His birthplace and the tribe of Israel into which He would be born. Some show that He would be betrayed for a certain amount of money, and even what that money would be used for afterward. This betrayal, as prophesied, would lead to His mistreatment and execution by men, and there are even more specific details about what occurs afterward.

Among these prophecies, there are many where the New Testament makes special mention of an Old Testament passage being fulfilled, effectively declaring that something happened in order that "the Scriptures may be fulfilled." For example, in Luke 24:44 Jesus stated that not only did the Old Testament bear witness to Him in a general way, but that in each of the three divisions of Old Testament Scripture—

the Law, the Prophets, and the Psalms, or Writings—there were things concerning Him. He added that all these things must be fulfilled. (See Matthew 1:22-23; 2:15, 17, 23; 4:14-16; 5:17; 8:17; 12:17-21; 13:14-15,35; 21:4-5; 26:54, 56; 27:9-10, 35; Mark 14:49; 15:28; Luke 4:21; 21:22; John 13:18; 15:25; 17:12; 19:24, 28, 36; Acts 1:16; 3:18; 13:27, 29, 33). The word "fulfill" means to bring to completion something that had been pledged earlier (see Jeremiah 44:25). As used in the New Testament, the idea is that what had been spoken in prophecy has now been accomplished.

Pious Jews of the first century regarded the Old Testament Scriptures with profound reverence, yet they recognized an incompleteness in them. Those Scriptures spoke of a day when God would judge the earth. They spoke of a King in David's lineage whose reign would be endless. They spoke of the nations of the world being blessed by Abraham and his descendants. They spoke of one like a Son of Man coming to Earth and receiving a Kingdom that will never be destroyed, and they described His power, glory, and judgment. They spoke of a prophet like Moses who would instruct the people with unparalleled teachings. They spoke of a servant of the Lord whose suffering would be intense and undeserved and whose death would bear away the sins of the people. They spoke of a Son of God whose character would measure up to that of His Father. This one who would come would fulfill the offices of prophet, priest, and king forever. Although He would be born of David's lineage, He would be of a humble, insignificant family. His birthplace would be Bethlehem. Not only would He restore the fallen in Israel; He would be a light to the Gentiles as well. He would be hated and rejected by the very people that He came to rescue from their bondage. He would die among criminals, and His tomb would be supplied by a rich man. But that would not be the last of Him. He would rise from the dead, and God's program would flourish in His hands. When He saw all that would be accomplished through His sufferings, He would rejoice, because through His death He sealed a new covenant between God and man. Indeed, His death would make it possible for ordinary men and women to have the Spirit of God come and take up residence within their lives.

Rather than list the hundreds of specific Old Testament prophecies pertaining to Jesus, let's follow a simple outline of the life of Christ and note some representative passages dealing with His person and work.

First, consider the *Messianic lineage.* The coming Savior and King will be the seed of Eve (Genesis 3:15); in the line of Seth (Genesis 4:25); through Noah (Genesis 6:9); a descendent of Abraham (Genesis 12:1-3); of the tribe of Judah (Genesis 49:10); of the House of David (2 Samuel 4:12, 13).

Look at predictions concerning the *birth of Christ.* He is to be born at Bethlehem (Micah 5:2); born of a virgin (Isaiah 7:14); worshipped by Gentiles (Isaiah 60:6).

Note prophecies of the *deity of Christ.* He is Immanuel, "God with us" (Isaiah 7:14); the Eternal Son (Psalm 2:7); the Mighty God, the Everlasting Father, the Prince of Peace (Isaiah 9:6, 7); the Great Prophet (Deuteronomy 18:15, 18); the Sovereign Scepter and the Morning Star (Numbers 24:17); the Divine Redeemer (Isaiah 59:20).

See prophecies concerning the *life of Christ.* He is to have a forerunner who will prepare for His public ministry (Isaiah 40:3; Malachi 3:1); He will fulfill the offices of Prophet (Deuteronomy 18:15-18); Priest (1 Samuel 2:35; Psalm 110:4); and King (2 Samuel 7:12-16; Psalm 2:7; Isaiah 9:6-7; Jeremiah 23:5-6); He will heal and save (Isaiah 61:1); He will be the Servant of Jehovah (Isaiah 42:1-7); He will present Himself as King riding on a donkey (Zechariah 9:9).

Consider prophecies concerning the d*eath of Christ*. He is to be deserted (Zechariah 13:7); spat upon (Isaiah 50:6); brutally beaten (Isaiah 52:14); but no bones will be broken (Psalm 34:20); He will be given vinegar to drink (Psalm 69:21). The Old Testament preview of the death of Christ is given especially in Isaiah 53 and Psalm 22. In Isaiah 53, His sufferings are for our sake and provide peace and healing (v. 5). He will be silent before His persecutors as a lamb led to the slaughter (v. 7). His soul will be an offering for sin (v. 10). He will die with the wicked but will be buried with the rich (v. 9). His sufferings are not because of His own sin, for He had none (v. 9). Isaiah gives an accurate and detailed account of the sufferings of Jesus and states the reason for His death. He died for the sins of others (v. 10-12).

In Psalm 22, part of which Jesus quoted while He was on the cross, the Messiah is to be forsaken of God (v. 1), ridiculed and taunted (v. 6-8); He will suffer unspeakable agony (v. 14-16); His bones will be pulled out of joint (v. 14); He will suffer thirst (v. 15); He will be pierced with nails (v. 16); His garments will be divided, with the exception of His vesture, for which they will cast lots (v. 18). This psalm presents a graphic picture of the crucifixion, the details of which were fulfilled by the events at Calvary.

Finally, see prophecies concerning the *resurrection and ascension of Christ*. Many passages anticipate His resurrection, but only a few are specific. Of these, the most important is Psalm 16:10, quoted by both Peter (Acts 2:25-31) and Paul (Acts 13:34-37). The ascension of Christ up to glory is the subject of Psalm 68:18.

This outline by no means exhausts the Old Testament prophecies concerning King Jesus. All of them came true in Him. There is no example in the literature of the whole world where the prophecies made centuries beforehand in a holy book were fulfilled in a historical person in this way. In fact, it is astronomically impossible that the prophecies of the Bible could be fulfilled apart from divine revelation. The prophecies concerning the Messiah amazed the followers of Jesus, but it convinced them. They saw in Him the fulfillment of these ancient prophecies, and they used them to make a tremendous impact on the events that followed.

Theophanies

Although our primary interest is to focus on the promises of the coming King to be found in the Old Testament, we must also emphasize the fact that Jesus is revealed in many ways throughout the Old Testament. Perhaps the clearest views of Christ in the Old Testament are found in the various theophanies. The word theophany comes from the Greek words *theos*, meaning "God," and *phaino*, meaning "to appear." Historically, the word refers to the various appearances of Christ in His pre-incarnate state. The most frequent theophany is the Angel of Jehovah, who is the Son of God appearing in the form of an angel. The references are too many to list, so let's notice a few representative passages.

Christ provides comfort to a disheartened Hagar (Genesis 16:7-13) and comes to her aid (Genesis 21:17-19). The Angel stays the hand of Abraham about to sacrifice Isaac and provides a substitute (Genesis 22:11-18). He goes before the servant of Abraham, seeking a wife for Isaac, and prospers his way (Genesis 27:7, 40). He ministers to Jacob (Genesis 31:11; 48:15-16). He appears to Moses in the burning bush to call him to work as a leader (Exodus 3:2). Throughout Exodus the Angel of

God is in the pillar of a cloud and a pillar of fire and leads Israel through the wilderness to the promised land. He warns Balaam (Numbers 22:22-35) and He warns and judges Israel (Judges 2:1-4). He instructs Gideon (Judges 6:11-23) and the parents of Samson (Judges 13:3-22). He converses with other people in various other places throughout the Old Testament. The angel judges sin, as in David's numbering Israel (2 Samuel 24:14-17; 1 Chronicles 21:11-30) and in the slaying of 185,000 Assyrians (2 Kings 19:35). He instructs Elijah (2 Kings 1:1-16) and Zechariah (Zechariah 1:9). He protects Daniel (Daniel 3:28; 6:22). There are many other theophanies in the Old Testament. In fact, we can safely assume that every visible manifestation of God in bodily form in the Old Testament is to be identified with the Lord Jesus Christ.

The theophanies reveal the Son of God to be exceedingly active in the Old Testament, judging sin, providing for people in need, protecting them from their enemies, guiding them in the path of God's will, and in general executing the providence of God. This picture of Jesus in the Old Testament is in complete harmony with the character and work of the King as revealed in the New Testament.

Types

Verses 6 and 11 of I Corinthians 10 state that certain events that took place in the history of Israel are types serving to instruct us. Verse 4 of the same chapter points to the rock in the wilderness as a type of Christ. The Old Testament contains many vivid pictures of Christ in the form of types. We may categorize them under five different headings: persons, events, things, institutions, and ceremonies. As with other Old Testament pronouncements pertaining to Christ, it's impossible in a brief discussion to consider all the revelations concerning Christ given in these types.

Therefore, we will simply summarize representative important types in these five groups and note their prophetic contributions.

Romans 5:12-21 contrasts the disobedience of Adam with the obedience of Christ. The passage presents Adam as a type of Christ since both stand at the head of the human race—Adam the head of the old humanity and Christ the head of the new (see also 1 Corinthians 15:45-47).

Melchizedek, described in Genesis 14:18-20 as king of Salem, is a type of Christ as Priest-King. Psalm 110:4 declares that Christ is a Priest forever after the order of Melchizedek, and Hebrews 5-7 builds heavily upon this prophecy in describing the eternal and superior priesthood of Christ. The name Melchizedek is significant. It's a combination of two words meaning "king" and "righteous," while Salem means "peace." Christ is the Eternal and Righteous King of Peace.

Joseph, loved by Israel more than all his other children, was hated and envied by his malicious brothers. They conspired against him to kill him, but then humiliated him by selling him into slavery. Later he was thrown into an Egyptian prison. Joseph was a type of Christ, despised and abused by wicked men. Then Joseph in his nobility, when Pharaoh made him ruler over Egypt, was a type of Christ whom God has highly exalted. Joseph is a figure of Christ as Beloved Son, Suffering Servant, and Gracious Sovereign.

Moses was a type of Christ as a prophet and as a deliverer from bondage. Joshua was a type of Christ because he was a conqueror. His name, which means "Jehovah saves," is the Old Testament equivalent of the Greek name Jehovah. David was a type of Christ first as shepherd and then as king. Samson was a type of Christ because of his strength to slay the lions and carry off the gates of impossibility. Solomon was a type of Christ because of the affluence of his reign. Jonah was a type of Christ because of his self-sacrifice for the rescue of others. In Genesis 22 the sacrifice of Isaac on Moriah is a foreshadowing of the death of Christ. Abel is a picture of Christ as the True Shepherd who made an acceptable bloody sacrifice to God in obedience to the command of God. Throughout the Old Testament, there is a constant reference to the kinsman-redeemer, in Hebrew *goel*. See, for instance, Leviticus 25:48-49 and the book of Ruth. These instances are a foreshadowing of Christ who would come to redeem through the sacrifice of Himself.

Many historical events bear witness to Christ. Noah's ark, with its one door, the only place where any living creature was safe from the destructive flood, pointed to Jesus, who said, "No one comes to the Father except through me" (John 14:6).

The Passover, with the lamb without blemish that was slain pointed in the forward direction to Christ and His crucifixion. The Bible declares, "Christ, our Passover, was sacrificed for us" (1 Corinthians 5:7). 1 Peter 1:18-19 reminds us: "You were not redeemed with corruptible things, like silver or gold . . . but with the precious blood of Christ, as of a lamb without blemish and without spot." The whole picture of Israel's deliverance out of Egypt, journey through the wilderness, and entrance into the promised land illustrates the work of Christ as the believer's safety from the judgment that overtakes the world. The manna that the people ate for 40 years portrays Christ as the Bread of Life. The rock that Moses struck to bring forth water speaks of the life-giving Christ. We are plainly told in 1 Corinthians 10:4, "That Rock was Christ." Crossing the Jordan River speaks of the death of Christ as the means of victory and entrance into the enjoyment of our present possessions in Christ, of which Canaan itself is a type.

Many things in the Old Testament foreshadow Christ. Aaron's rod that budded typifies Christ's resurrection. Numbers 17 records how Moses made a serpent of brass and set it upon a pole, and anyone who had been bitten by snakes could look at it and be healed. In the serpent we see the symbol of sin; in the brass, we see judgment upon sin. The brazen serpent represents Christ, who was made to be sin for us (2 Corinthians 5:21). Jesus said to Nicodemus, "As Moses lifted up the serpent in the wilderness, even so must the Son of Man be lifted up" (John 3:14).

The Tabernacle is an almost inexhaustible source of illustrations of spiritual truths relating to Jesus, speaking of Him in every phase of His ministry—His person, sacrifice, intercession, and provision for those who trust in Him. The Bible says that the Lord "became flesh and dwelt (literally *tabernacled*) among us" (John 1:14). The wood of the Tabernacle speaks of the humanity of Christ; the gold of the Tabernacle speaks of the deity of Christ; the veil in the Tabernacle speaks of the flesh of Christ; the altar speaks of the sacrifice of Christ.

The entire Jewish ceremonial system, with its sacrifices and feasts, speaks of the atonement wrought by Jesus. Almost every aspect of the meaning of the death of Jesus is anticipated in the various Old Testament sacrifices. Central in the sacrifices is the feature of shed blood, looking forward to the sacrifice of Christ. God tells us in Leviticus 17:11: "For the life of the flesh is in the blood, and I have given it to you upon the altar to make atonement for your souls, for it is the blood that makes atonement for the soul."

The offering of an unblemished lamb was the most common sacrifice, prefiguring "the Lamb of God who takes away the sin of the world" (John 1:29). The lamb speaks of the purity of Christ (1 Peter 1:19), the gentleness and submission of Christ to the will of God (Acts 8:32; 1

Peter 2:21-23), and the substitutionary death of Jesus, bearing sin that was not His own. The book of Revelation repeatedly refers to Jesus as "the Lamb."

In order to understand properly the significance of the sacrifice, you should study carefully the book of Hebrews, particularly chapters 9 and 10. Taken as a whole, the animal sacrifices were bloody fingers of prophecy pointing to the one sacrifice of Christ as forever putting away sin. The sacrifices were elemental; they were preparatory; they were rudimentary; they were introductory. They all pointed to Christ. The book of Hebrews also explains the priesthood of Christ, of which both the priesthoods of Aaron and Melchizedek were types.

We cannot overestimate the importance of feasts in Israel's religious life. They were the backbone of the Levitical system and most of them have a definite typical meaning in relation to Christ. They are outlined in Leviticus 23.

We have already seen how Jesus fulfilled the spiritual meaning of the Passover, the first and in some respects the most important feast. The second feast, the Feast of Unleavened Bread, which immediately followed the Passover, speaks of Christ as the Bread of Life, the holy walk of believers after redemption, and the believer's communion with Christ.

The Feast of Firstfruits celebrates the new harvest in the land and typifies the resurrection of Christ. The Bible says, "But now Christ is risen from the dead, and has become the firstfruits of those who have fallen asleep. . . But each one in his own order: Christ the firstfruits, afterward those who are Christ's at His coming" (1 Corinthians 15:21, 23).

The Feast of the Wave Loaves, coming exactly 50 days after the Feast of Firstfruits, foreshadowed the day of Pentecost, when believers experienced the outpouring of the Holy Spirit.

The Day of Atonement represents the work of Christ on the cross. The ceremonies involved two goats. One of them was killed, and the High Priest took its blood into the Holy of Holies and sprinkled it upon the mercy seat. This act pictured Christ as our propitiation. The other goat was driven into the wilderness after the sins of the people were symbolically transferred to it. This act is the origin of the English word scapegoat, one who bears blame for others. The ceremony depicts Christ as our substitute, bearing our sins upon Himself.

The Feast of Tabernacles commemorated the wandering of Israel in the wilderness, reminding us of our temporary pilgrimage on this earth.

In the Old Testament, six cities were designated as "cities of refuge" to provide a sanctuary for those who innocently had taken the life of another. Those cities were a type of Christ, in whom sinners find refuge from judgment.

All Bible types are so related to Christ that He alone explains them, and Jesus alone is the vital substance that gives meaning to the Bible's genealogies, its histories, and chronologies.

The Fullness of the Time

Jesus did not enter a world unprepared for His coming. Within the changing tides of history, God had been producing His history. Galatians 4:4 states, "When the fullness of the time had come, God sent forth His Son." In other words, it was when world conditions were exactly right for His coming that Jesus came. There never has been in history any other generation better suited for the coming of Jesus than the generation in which He did come. The same God who planted the gospel prepared the soil. Various individuals, institutions, and nations were His servants and instruments then and now, whether conscious of it or not. Even the pagan world helped to make possible the divine purpose of God.

Political Preparation

Under the control of Rome, there was *political unity* in the world. In the first century, the Roman Empire embraced all the territory from the Euphrates River to the Atlantic Ocean, and from the Danube River and the southern borders of Scotland to the Sahara Desert. The world, so to speak, was one big community. The triumph of Roman armies had established the *Pax Romana*, a reference to a roughly 200-year-long timespan of Roman history that began with Augustus, who became the emperor in 24 B.C. Under his reign, one of the world's most efficient organizations was perfected, with a resulting era of peace, security, and progress.

The world into which Christ came was one in which Rome with an iron hand preserved and enforced law and order. The Mediterranean Sea, so long plagued and plundered by pirates, was cleared of this menace by government ships. Over this body of water, except in the cold of winter, ships sailed to keep the various peoples of the empire in constant touch with each other.

Because of the vastness of the Roman Empire, there was a need to connect strategically important cities and territories for military, administrative, and commercial purposes. Therefore, Roman engineers crisscrossed the empire with thousands of miles of *excellently constructed highways*. The old saying, "All roads lead to Rome," was literally true. You can still visit and walk on many of them all over the Mediterranean region and lands beyond. Because of the highways and because the empire was relatively peaceful, safe travel was possible, allowing the early Christian missionaries to spread the gospel. Such freedom to travel would have been impossible in other eras.

Thanks to the conquests of Alexander the Great, there was a *universal language* that was spoken for a period of at least 500 years, beginning in 330 B.C. This language was known as *koine* ("common") Greek, because of two reasons. First, it sprung up as a common language among troops of the prolific conqueror and it was spoken in the many countries they conquered, spreading all the way from Egypt to India. Another reason for the name *koine* is to distinguish the language from the classical Greek used in writing literature and poetry. *Koine* is the common vernacular that ordinary citizens would use in communicating with each other in their homes and in public. Hence, it was much simplified for everyday conversation. The New Testament is written in *koine* Greek, as well as the Septuagint, the Greek translation of the Old Testament. It was certainly by divine providence that those documents were written in a language that the people could readily understand. Were it not for this common language, the books of the New Testament probably would have been written in a variety of different languages, and they would not have been accessible to everyone without a translation. Furthermore, a common language made it much easier for the early Christian evangelists to communicate the gospel to people in other parts of the world. More important than serving as a universal vehicle of communication, the Greek of the New Testament is a remarkably precise and explicit language, probably the most expressive of all time. The vocabulary, grammar, and syntax of *koine* Greek allows for precise and subtle distinctions between various forms of expression. In other words, it can express a message clearly, with pinpoint accuracy that is easily understandable.

Economic Preparation

Throughout the Roman Empire in the first century, there was *widespread destitution.* For the most part, the middle class had vanished. Historians record that Roman society may have consisted of a handful of wealthy individuals that made up 0.6% of the population, an army that made up 0.4% of the population, and the poor masses that made up 99% of the populace. Idleness was prevalent, leading to all kinds of evil. These grim conditions caused people to long for something better. Roman society rested on the foundation of *slavery.* Slaves outnumbered free people in Rome by three to one. Conservative estimates place the number of slaves in the first-century Roman Empire at 60,000,000, and their condition was most wretched, for they had neither protection nor right. The Roman world was ready for a message of hope and deliverance.

Moral Preparation

The first chapter of Paul's letter to the Romans pictures a world sunk in moral hopelessness. There was such widespread debauchery that even pagan writers of the day described the world as pursuing its riotous way down to disaster and oblivion. The philosopher Seneca lamented, "Vice no longer hides itself; it stalks forth before all eyes. Innocence is not only rare but nowhere." Immoral behavior of whatever fashion, including total depravity, was acceptable. Abortion and infanticide were very common. A newborn baby would be brought to the *pater familias,* the father, who would decide if the child was to be kept, sold to slave traffickers, thrown out with the trash, exposed in the market place, or killed. One of the most common ways to dispose of an unwanted child was to throw the baby into the Tiber River. A letter, dating from 1 B.C., from a man traveling in Egypt to his pregnant wife in Rome demonstrates the casual view of infanticide. He wishes her a safe delivery and then comments, "If it is a boy, let it live; if it is a girl, kill it." Infidelity in marriage was the norm. The typical attitude toward marriage is revealed by a Roman nobleman: "We have wives to bear us legitimate children; we have mistresses for the sake of pleasure; we have concubines for the daily care of our persons."

However, amid a society where there were no moral restraints, there remained a sense of decency, and many people were ready to hear and respond to a gospel that offered salvation and a new life of holiness lived above the degradation that surrounded them.

Religious Preparation

The world of the first century was characterized by a spiritual dearth. Morally and spiritually the Greco-Roman world of the first century was bankrupt. The pagan religions of the empire were impotent, if not already dead. The forms continued to exist, but their power was gone. Their gods were too much like mortals to be taken seriously. Magic, astrology, philosophy, and mystical ceremonies left only dissatisfaction and disillusionment, and belief in fate and destiny was heavily oppressive. Overall, pagan religion left nothing but widespread disgust with life and deep-seated pessimism.

Positively, however, there is abundant evidence of the deep hunger of heart that people of that century and the empire had for spiritual truth. Many philosophers not only led the people to see the folly of their belief in the many gods that they worshiped, but they also pointed the way to a higher concept of the supreme being and of the universe. In reality, the world was crying for God. That cry is well expressed in the words of Seneca: "Where shall he be found whom we have been seeking so many centuries?" There was an air of expectancy as people in their moral, economic, and religious destitution dared hope for something better. For this reason, the first Kingdom ambassadors who preached the gospel of Jesus Christ found a ready audience among the Gentiles.

Jewish Preparation

We have already discussed the many prophecies of the Messiah in the Old Testament and the passionate hopes of the Jews for His coming. Foreign oppression and economic deprivation intensified those hopes, even though they had developed some mistaken notions concerning their deliverer. It's true that for the most part, the Jews rejected Jesus as their King-Messiah, but the few who wholeheartedly followed Him changed the course of history.

The fact that Jews were scattered far outside the boundaries of Palestine provided the Gentiles with a knowledge of monotheism and they themselves became an audience for Christian missionaries to preach the gospel. The diaspora, or the Jewish dispersion among the Gentiles, began with the Babylonian captivity in the sixth century B.C., when many Jews voluntarily chose to remain in foreign lands. By the first century, Jewish communities had sprung up all over the Roman Empire, and an estimated 5,000,000 Jews lived outside Palestine, numbering far more than those in Palestine. However, Jews of the dispersion still looked to Palestine as the center of their religious and cultural life. Jewish law decreed that there must be a synagogue in any village where there were at least ten adult Jews. Whenever the first Christian missionaries, who were all Jews, entered a town, they would go first to the synagogue.

After his conquest of Egypt, Alexander, who was favorable to the Jews, allotted a portion of the new city of Alexandria to Jews who wanted to settle there. Many Jews did indeed reside in Alexandria, and in the third century B.C., they translated the Hebrew Scriptures into *koine* Greek, making the Old Testament available to the entire Gentile world. This translation is known as the Septuagint (Seventy) because 70 rabbis did the translation.

This is the "fullness of the time" that God had providentially prepared for the coming of the King.

THE BIRTH OF THE KING

History's greatest happening was when God came to earth in the form of a baby boy named Jesus. Here is the hinge on which history turns, the dividing point between old and new, the single event that gives meaning to all other events. With all due respect to all the learned people of this world, although they may be highly educated and intelligent, it's my conclusion that if they do not understand this event, they don't have the key to knowledge. It's sad for one to know biology, the study of life, and not know Jesus Christ, the giver of life. It's sad for one to know geology and the composition and the strata of rocks, and not know Jesus Christ, the Rock of Ages. It's sad for one to know astronomy, to identify the stars and chart the galaxies, and not know Jesus Christ, the Bright and Morning Star. It's sad for one to know botany and be able to name and explain the composition of every flower, and not know Jesus Christ, the Rose of Sharon who can fragrance any life. It's sad for one to know history from its very beginning and to miss the central event in all of history, His story.

The cornerstone of our faith is that in the birth of Jesus God became man, and He did so without giving up His deity. Why did God become man, and how did He become man? He did it for two reasons— to reveal Himself and to redeem us by paying the penalty for our sins on the cross. God exists in a realm that no human being can understand, so He translated Himself into a word that we can understand, and the name of that word is Jesus. For an elaboration of that statement, review the earlier comments on John 1:1 and Hebrews 1:1-2. The great mystery of the manger is that God translated deity into humanity without discarding the deity or distorting the humanity. God became flesh, and He did it through the virgin birth of Jesus. Isaiah 7:14, quoted in Matthew 1:23, tells about the conception of Jesus: "Therefore the Lord Himself will give you a sign: Behold, the virgin shall conceive and bear a Son, and shall call His name Immanuel." If you say that you don't understand how that's possible, I reply that I don't either and I don't know anyone who does. The Bible says in 1 Timothy 3:16, "And without controversy great is the mystery of godliness: God was manifested in the flesh." Even the mother of Jesus thought it was impossible. When the angel Gabriel told her what was going to happen, Mary responded, "How can this be?" The angel gave the best and only explanation: "With God, nothing will be impossible" (Luke 1:26-38). The miracle of the ages is the virgin conception of the Lord Jesus Christ.

During His public ministry, the enemies of Jesus sought to discredit Him by spreading rumors about the illegitimacy of His birth. For example, when Jesus declared that certain unbelieving Jews had the devil as their father instead of Abraham, they retorted, "We were not born of fornication," a strong innuendo that He was (John 8:39-47). On one occasion in His own hometown, as recorded in Mark 6:3, the people were offended by His teaching, and asked contemptuously, "Isn't this the son of Mary?" This was a deliberate insult, and the insinuation would not have been missed. Then on another occasion, unbelievers shouted at the man born blind, whom Jesus had healed, "We know that God spoke to Moses; as for this fellow, we do not know where he is from" John

8:29). These rumors of illegitimacy became even more explicit in the Jewish Talmud, which describes the birth of Jesus as the result of Mary's adultery.

Anyone who has difficulty believing in the virgin birth has difficulty believing in God. Why have difficulty believing that a child could come into this world without an earthly father when God made the first man and the first woman out of nothing? Anyone who believes Genesis 1:1 shouldn't have difficulty believing in any miracle.

Anyone who doubts the virgin birth doubts the Bible. No one can honestly deny that the Bible plainly teaches the virgin birth, so the question is not whether the Bible teaches the virgin birth, but whether the Bible is true or false. We must therefore face the question frankly. If the Bible contains myth or falsehood, then it's completely unreliable, and biblical authority is gone. The Bible stands or falls as a whole. No individual or committee has the competency to say that certain parts of the Bible are true and therefore to be accepted, but other parts are untrue and therefore to be rejected. If you deny the virgin birth, then you deny the authority of the Bible.

Furthermore, to deny the virgin birth is to deny the deity of Jesus. If Jesus was not born of a virgin, then He was a descendant of Adam, just like we all are, and He was a sinner by nature and a sinner by practice. Those who don't believe in the virgin birth need to read 1 John 5:10: "He who does not believe God has made Him a liar." It's seriously frightening to call God a liar.

Why is the virgin birth of Jesus Christ so important, and why do we emphasize it? The simple answer is that the deity of Jesus is wrapped up in His virgin birth. Many people teach that even assuming that the virgin birth is factual, it is not vital for faith. That assertion is not valid, because faith itself rests on valid facts. If something is important, that which makes it possible is also of vital importance. If Joseph was the father of Jesus, then He was the product of the human race and He was not sinless. And if He is not sinless, then He cannot be our Savior who died for our sins as a sinless substitute. No virgin birth, no sinless Christ. No sinless Christ, no atonement. No atonement, no forgiveness. No forgiveness, no hope of heaven. No hope of heaven, we die and go to hell. Take away the virgin birth and the whole house of Christianity collapses like a house of cards.

The birth of Jesus was unique, miraculous, and divine. In His birth, *God* came into the world, and that is something quite beyond a biological fact. It can neither be proved nor disapproved by science. It is rather something to be believed or disbelieved. There is no proof, only testimony, and God testifies to its truth in His Word. The supernatural birth of Jesus is the alpha of our Christian faith. Accept it and the whole alphabet follows as a matter of course. Deny it and, like a planet that leaves its orbit, there is no telling where unbelief will carry you.

We have seen that the Old Testament repeatedly promises a King who will reign victoriously forever over His Kingdom. We have also seen the fulfillment of that fulfillment in Jesus Christ (see Hebrews 1:8). In his Gospel, Matthew presents the genealogy of Jesus, which clearly shows that He is the One who has the right and title to the Davidic throne, and records the supernatural birth of Jesus, which qualifies Him as being truly the fulfillment of the Old Testament prophecies concerning the King. Seven hundred years before the birth of Jesus, the prophet Isaiah vividly described His supernatural birth:

For unto us a Child is born,

Unto us a Son is given;

And the government will be upon His shoulder.

And His name will be called

Wonderful, Counselor, Mighty God,

Everlasting Father, Prince of Peace.

Of the increase of His government and peace

There will be no end,

Upon the throne of David and over His kingdom,

To order it and establish it with judgment and justice

From that time forward, even forever.

The zeal of the Lord of hosts will perform this.

--Isaiah 9:6-7

This passage speaks of the mystery of the humanity of Jesus ("a Child is born") and the majesty of His deity ("a Son is given"). The baby was the Son of God and God the Son. He was as much God as if He were not man at all, and as much man as if He were not God at all. The passage focuses on the sovereign nobility of the baby. "The government will be upon His shoulder." He is the ruler. He was born a king. He came not only to redeem; He came to reign. "The zeal of the Lord of hosts will perform this," that is, Almighty God has put all His divine energy into seeing that this is done.

The King's name is Wonderful. Matthew 1:21 reveals that God the Father gave the baby the name Jesus. Mary did not think up the name, nor did Joseph. Through the angel Gabriel, God named the baby. The reason for the name is that "He will save His people from their sins." The name Jesus literally means "Jehovah saves." Jehovah is the most sacred name for God in the Hebrew Bible. As we have seen, it means the great I AM. "There never was a time when I was not; there never will be a time when I will not be." That was the name of the baby born to the virgin Mary. In His birth, He was wonderful. In His life, He was wonderful. In His works, He was wonderful. In His death, He was wonderful. In His resurrection, He was wonderful. In His ascension, He was wonderful. In His intercession, He is wonderful. When He comes again, He will be wonderful.

The King's name is Counselor. There is wisdom in the King's name. The Bible says that in Jesus "are hidden all the treasures of wisdom and knowledge" (Colossians 2:3). Godless society has rejected that wisdom in preference to its own foolishness, with the result that the world is in its present situation and doesn't know what to do about it.

The King's name is Mighty God. We have already shown evidence for the deity of Jesus and the worship due to Him. The word "mighty" denotes the King's leadership role. In the original Hebrew, the word means "having or showing great power and authority as a leader; heroic, valiant." In every aspect of His life and ministry, Jesus demonstrated divine power and authority. He began His public ministry "in the power of the Spirit, and news of him went out through all the surrounding region" (Luke 4:14). People testified that Jesus was "a Prophet mighty in deed and word before God and all the people" (Luke 24:19). His mighty works showed that "the power of the Lord was present to heal them" (Luke 5:17). As people touched Jesus, "power went out from him and healed them all" (Luke 6:19; see Luke 8:46).

When Jesus cast out demons, He proved that He is both divine and mighty, operating under God's complete authority and power (Luke 4:36). Peter proclaimed to the people of Israel that God attested Jesus to them "by miracles, wonders, and signs which God did through Him" (Acts 2:22). Christ's supernatural acts confirmed that He is Mighty God.

The most convincing proof that Jesus is Mighty God is the resurrection (Romans 1:4). Jesus had the power to lay down His life and take it up again (John 10:18), and God demonstrated "His mighty power which He worked in Christ when He raised Him from the dead and seated Him at His right hand in the heavenly places" (Ephesians 1:19-20).

The King's name is Everlasting Father. Jesus said, "I and My Father are one" (John 10:30), and "He who has seen Me has seen the Father" (John 14:9).

The King's name is Prince of Peace. At His birth, a multitude of angels proclaimed, "Glory to God in the highest, and on earth peace, goodwill toward men" (Luke 2:14). The reality of that proclamation awaits the King's return, but meanwhile, "having been justified by faith, we have peace with God through our Lord Jesus Christ" (Romans 5:1). The Prince of Peace shows us that He can bring peace wherever He rules. He can bring us peace in life's trials (John 14:27); peace as we grow in Him (1 Thessalonians 5:23); peace in spiritual battles (Romans 16:20); peace with one another (Ephesians 4:2); peace as we submit to the Holy Spirit (Galatians 5:22).

God loved us so much that He sent Jesus into the world, not only to reveal Himself to us but to teach us how to live and to provide a way of escape from sin's tyranny, as His name indicates. He was born to die. He said that He didn't come to be served, but to serve and give

His life a ransom for many (Mark 10:45). Jesus repeatedly referred to the crucifixion as that vital hour for which He came into the world (John 2:4; 23:23, 27; 13:1; 17:1; see 7:30; 8:20).

THE TEACHINGS OF THE KING

`Whenever, wherever, and whatever Jesus taught, people got excited. Even the demons got riled up and the religious leaders got angry. In the end, it got Him killed on a Roman cross. What exactly was this inspiring, challenging, goading, and apparently subversive message of Jesus all about? We have already emphasized that the core of Jesus' message, as stated in Mark 1:15, is, briefly and simply, "The kingdom of God is at hand." But the people weren't ready yet for the kingdom because they hadn't yet understood their need for the righteousness that the King would provide. Because of that lack of understanding and the arrival of the King, there was a need for someone to prepare them for both the King and the message He would bring.

The Ministry of John the Baptist

In ancient times a herald would go ahead of the king to prepare for his arrival and to announce his coming. Malachi 3:1 is a prophecy that a messenger would come who would prepare the way for Israel's Messiah. The Messiah's coming would signal the arrival of the King and the beginning of the Messianic Kingdom. However, the voice of prophecy had been silent for 400 years. But now it sounds again, because about 28 years after the birth of Jesus, "there was a man sent from God, whose name was John" (John 1:6). Matthew 3:1 describes his coming: "In those days John the Baptist came preaching in the wilderness of Judea." His ministry was not his idea. He did not suddenly for some reason decide to be a prophet. "The word of God came to John" (Luke 3:2). There is one word that describes his ministry, and that word is "preaching" (Matthew 3:1; Mark 1:4; Luke 3:3). That one-word description is very vivid. It literally means to act as a herald, and that's exactly what John was. He was the herald going before the King, shouting His arrival and proclaiming the message that God had given him (Matthew 11:9-10). His was "the voice of one crying in the wilderness" (Mark 1:3). Notice that John the Baptist was a voice, not an echo. He did not hesitate to say exactly what God gave him to say, not what the public wanted to hear. A statement that Jesus made concerning John shows the importance of his ministry and its impact upon the people. Jesus said, "Assuredly I say to you, among those born of women there has not risen one greater than John the Baptist" (Matthew 11:11).

The challenge both John the Baptist and Jesus faced was that the Jews believed that being Jewish was all that mattered. They trusted in their ancestry for salvation. They thought that because they were descendants of Abraham, they were assured of entrance into the Kingdom of heaven. John the Baptist forcefully rejected salvation for the Jews based on their ancestry. He declared, "God is able to raise up children to Abraham from these stones" (Matthew 3:9). The Jewish religious leaders also taught that righteousness consisted in outward obedience to the laws God had given Israel through Moses. John, called for the people to repent and to change their minds about how a person becomes part of the Kingdom. Jesus later made the same demand of the people. Their self-perceived righteousness was not enough. Their heritage and works were not what God required. Instead, God required that the people have a true, internal righteousness that they didn't yet possess. Not only did they need a

King, but they needed a Savior.

The outward symbol of repentance was baptism. The Jews practiced baptism, but it was only for Gentiles who converted to Judaism. They felt that they themselves had no need to be baptized, so for them to submit to baptism was a very radical step. Those who were baptized were admitting that being a descendant of Abraham was not enough, that leading a good life was not enough, and that observing rites and ceremonies was not enough. By repentance and baptism, they were renouncing all dependence on religious privilege, casting themselves on the mercy of God, and preparing to meet the Messiah when He came.

The Kingdom of God

We have emphasized the fact that the Kingdom of God is the heart of what Jesus taught. In fact, not only was it the central message that He preached, but it was also the one He sent His disciples to preach, and I might add, to live. As I averred at the very beginning, if we don't get the message of the Kingdom of God, then we don't get the gospel at all. It's difficult for us to imagine the stir that Jesus caused when He made the announcement that with Him came the arrival of the Kingdom. Everyone was eagerly longing for the coming of the Kingdom but of course, they had a different interpretation of it. For most of the Jews, the Kingdom meant the day that God would step in on behalf of His oppressed people, defeat the hated Romans, and establish His rule.

Remember that the message of Jesus about the Kingdom and His call to repentance was a direct sequel to John's call to radical change. Their message was the same, and John had pointed to Jesus as the Messiah. No wonder there was such excitement! The crowds materialized from everywhere and gathered around Jesus. Surely this would be the time for the decisive defeat of the Roman conquerors. But instead of talking about a military campaign, Jesus stood in His home synagogue in Nazareth and read a portion of Isaiah:

> "The Spirit of the Lord is upon Me, because He has anointed
> Me to preach the gospel to the poor; He has sent Me to heal the
> brokenhearted, to proclaim liberty to the captives
> and recovery of sight to the blind, to set at liberty those who are
> oppressed; to proclaim
> the acceptable year of the Lord" (Luke 4:18-19).

To the amazement of the people, He added, "Today this Scripture is fulfilled in your hearing" (Luke 4:21). Instead of rebellion against Rome, Jesus concentrated on the spiritual aspects of the Old Testament hope. So, what were the features of the Kingdom that He came to inaugurate? Actually, everything He taught concerns an aspect of the Kingdom. We find a summary of His version of the Kingdom in His most famous address, which we know as The Sermon on the Mount (Matthew 5-7). I think of it as The Kingdom Manifesto, because in this teaching Jesus explicitly told what the Kingdom of God is all about and what it looks like.

He began with a prescription for a happy life in the Kingdom when we follow the King's instructions. Then He goes on to spell out what it means and what it takes. It's a life of attractive goodness, totally different from the legalistic ethics taught by their religious leaders. It will be like salt adding savor to food or like light to people stumbling around in the darkness. In contrast to religious people who make a show of their piety in order to impress others, who give offerings to be praised by others, and who pray to be seen by others, in the Kingdom secret prayer, unseen generosity, and unostentatious worship is the order of the day. People in the Kingdom realize that the thought or the desire is the father of the deed. Therefore, hatred is as obnoxious to God as murder, and lust as adultery. Divorce is not the way for Kingdom citizens. God made the man and the woman in marriage to be and to remain one flesh. Everything else is a fall from that ideal. There is no need in the Kingdom for flowery oaths. In the Kingdom, your word is your bond. You should not judge others but consider your own faults and shortcomings. You are to strive to be the best version of yourself and serve God in all you do. Forgiveness is your way of life, even when you have been wronged. Love, even love for one's enemies, is characteristic of the Kingdom. You are displaying the character of our King when you love and forgive.

Life in the Kingdom of God is characterized by modesty, generosity, and prayer. There is no need to parade your piety and draw attention to yourself. People in the Kingdom won't hoard their money but will be generous in giving, thus making investments in heaven. They will be single-hearted in their devotion to and dependence upon the King, and they will enjoy marvelous peace. They realize that worrying about things is a mark of heathens and it accomplishes nothing. After all, the King looks after birds and flowers, so we can trust Him to look after us. When we make the Kingdom of God our priority, the King will take care of the material needs. However, we don't just take things for granted in our relationship with the King. We must ask, seek, and knock. You must enter the Kingdom through a narrow gate, and you must build your life on the rock of Jesus.

This is only a brief summary of what life in the Kingdom is all about, as described by Jesus. It was a revolutionary teaching that angered hypocritical religious leaders but attracted earnest seekers of the truth.

Jesus not only described the Kingdom of God as a present reality, initiated with His life and work; He also viewed the Kingdom in terms of a future dimension. The King is now ruling, but His Kingdom is not fully manifest. The Kingdom is coming to a consummation, described by Jesus in apocalyptic imagery that is recorded in Matthew 24. Christ's Second Coming will be the culmination of the Kingdom and the ushering in of the eternal Kingdom. All the hopes of the Old Testament prophets will be fulfilled. There will be a new heaven and a new earth, where justice and peace will reign, and God's will indeed be done. The dead will be judged, and their final destiny will be determined. Nobody knows when that day will come, so until then disciples of the Lord must be alert and faithfully serve Him.

The Holy Spirit

One of the most important areas of the teaching of Jesus concerns the person and work of the Holy Spirit. Jesus made clear His own consciousness of the Spirit's part in His mission. He said, "If I cast out demons by the Spirit of God, surely the kingdom of God has come upon you" (Matthew 12:28). At the beginning of His ministry Jesus applied the prophecy of Isaiah 61:1-2 to Himself, evidencing His own specific claim to the Spirit's power (Luke 4:18-19). When He was accused of casting out demons by Beelzebub, the ruler of the demons, Jesus replied by showing the true nature of this charge as a blasphemy against the Holy Spirit. This is unforgivable, although blasphemy against Jesus Himself as Son of Man may be forgiven. In a striking way, Jesus brought out the sovereign character of the Spirit's work (Matthew 12:22-32). Jesus promised the Spirit's guidance when the disciples must answer for their faith (Matthew 10:19-20). He promised the Spirit to those who ask the heavenly Father (Luke 11:13). In His conversation with Nicodemus, Jesus revealed the Spirit as the agent of regeneration (John 3:1-8). Without His activity, there can be no rebirth. Jesus, speaking of the Holy Spirit, promised that rivers of living waters would flow from those who come to Him (John 7:38-39).

The teachings of Jesus concerning the Holy Spirit become more explicit in the Upper Room discourses (John 14-17). He promised that the Holy Spirit would *restore the presence of Jesus* "in" us, not merely "with" us: "I will pray the Father and He will give you another Helper, that He may abide with you forever--the Spirit of truth, whom the world cannot receive, because it neither sees Him nor knows Him, but you know Him, for He dwells with you and will be in you. I will not leave you orphans; I will come to you" (John 14:16-18). In the Old Testament, the Spirit was a presence "with" people and occasionally came "upon" anointed people, but now He will be "in" us. The word "abide" means that He will dwell permanently in us. In the Greek language, there are two different words for "another." One (*allos*) means another of the same kind, and the other one (*heteros*) means another of a different kind. For example, suppose you have a car of a certain make and model, and you say, "I'm going to buy another car." If you use the one word, you are going to buy a car exactly like the one you have. If you use the other word, you are going to buy a car of a different make and model. When Jesus said that He would send another Helper, He used the word for the same kind, meaning that someone just like Him was going to come. The Holy Spirit is Christ in the Christian. In this passage, we see the Trinity. Notice that in verse 16 Jesus said that the Father would send them "another Helper," while in verse 18 he said, "I will come." They are the same. Earlier, in verses 7-11, Jesus said that the apostles knew the Father because they knew the Son. Now, He said that they also knew the Spirit because they knew the Son. Each Person of the Trinity is eternally distinct from the others, as seen by the fact that the Son can speak of the Father and of the Spirit as being each a separate *He.* Yet, the three Persons are so completely one in their essential being that to know one is to know the others. Jesus even said that it's impossible to know the Son without thereby knowing the Father and the Son as well.

All of us have probably looked upon the disciples with envy, wishing that we could have walked and talked with Jesus, heard Him teach the multitudes, watched as He healed the sick and raised the dead, and performed other miracles. That kind of aspiration is natural, but it's mistaken. We have the advantage over those who knew Him only in the flesh. Jesus said to the apostles, "It is to your advantage that I go away, for if I do not go away, the Helper will not come to you; but if I depart I will send Him to you" (John 16:7). It's better because when Jesus was on earth in the flesh, He could be located only in one geographical place at one time. And if He was in one spot, He couldn't be in another spot at the same time. The Spirit makes Christ available to us continuously and universally. Jesus emphasized this reality by telling the apostles that through the Spirit He would be with them "forever," and that He would no longer be merely "with" them but "in" them (John 14:16-17). Those who have the indwelling of the Holy Spirit no longer enjoy the presence of Jesus spasmodically or temporarily but without interruption or end.

The Holy Spirit would also be sent to *represent the person of Jesus* to us. "The Helper, the Holy Spirit, whom the Father will send in My name, He will teach you all things, and bring to your remembrance all things that I said to you" (John 14:26). The word "Helper," or in some versions, "Comforter," translates the Greek word *paracletos*, usually transliterated "paraclete." Literally, the word means "one called alongside to help," and it's the word for an advocate, one who represents someone and pleads his case before a judge. That's the way it's used in 1 John 2:1: "If anyone sins, we have an Advocate with the Father, Jesus Christ the righteous." The same word is used for the Holy Spirit four times in John's Gospel and for Jesus once in his first epistle. So, every Christian is related to two advocates, the Holy Spirit and Jesus Christ. But in what way?

Notice first the advocacy of Jesus in 1 John 2:1. Jesus is your advocate who represents you to the Father. Satan is called the "accuser of the brethren" (Zechariah 3:1-2; Job 2:1-6; Revelation 12:10). He is like a prosecuting attorney, and he accuses you before the Judge, God the Father, of all your sins. But when the devil accuses you, you "have an Advocate with the Father, Jesus Christ the Righteous." Your Advocate takes your case and pleads your cause to the Father. He doesn't plead innocence; He doesn't plead justifiable causes; He doesn't plead temporary insanity; He admits your guilt. He says, "Father, it's true that this person sinned, but I paid the penalty for his sins on the cross, and when he confessed and repented of his sins, I put them under my blood and cleansed him." There can be only one verdict— "justified!" So, when the devil gets on your case and pronounces condemnation against you, you can just say, "See my lawyer!"

Jesus is our Advocate who represents us to the Father, and the Holy Spirit is our Advocate who represents Jesus to us. He takes the things of Jesus Christ and makes them known to us. Jesus said in John 15:26, "But when the Helper comes, whom I shall send to you from the Father, the Spirit of truth who proceeds from the Father, He will testify of Me." The Holy Spirit pleads the cause of Jesus to us. It is only through His representation that we can really know Jesus Christ. The Bible elaborates on this fact in 1 Corinthians 2:9-16. Notice verse 9: "Eye has not seen, nor ear heard, nor have entered into the heart of man the things which God has prepared for those who love Him." This verse is often quoted at funerals, with the thought that when we get to heaven, we will know all these wonderful things. That may be true, but that isn't the meaning of this verse. You don't have to wait until you get to heaven to understand spiritual truths. You don't understand them with your natural abilities, "but God has revealed them to us through His Spirit. For the Spirit searches all things, yes, the deep things of God" (verse 10). Just as only the spirit of a person knows what's going on in the mind of the person, only the Spirit of God knows the thoughts of God. And

God has revealed those things through the Holy Spirit. The following verses point out that it's impossible for people without the Holy Spirit to understand spiritual things. What you can't learn with your physical faculties or with the emotions of your heart, you can know when the Holy Spirit of God makes those things real to you.

The Holy Spirit also makes Christ known to you; He pleads the cause of Christ (John 15:26). Jesus promised, "When He, the Spirit of truth, has come, He will guide you into all truth: for He will not speak on His own authority, but whatever He hears He will speak; and He will tell you things to come. He will glorify Me, for He will take of what is Mine and declare it to you. All things that the Father has are Mine. Therefore I said that He will take of Mine and declare it to you" (John 16:13-15). The Holy Spirit represents Christ to us.

The Holy Spirit will *recall the teachings of Jesus* for us. He will "bring to your remembrance all things that I said to you" (John 14:26). Not only does the Holy Spirit quicken your mind to learn the truth but He quickens your mind to recall the truth. The first fulfillment of this promise was to the apostles, as seen in the writing of the New Testament, particularly the Gospels. However, the Bible makes it clear that the Holy Spirit will bring to our remembrance the exact Scripture needed for a particular situation. For example, in times of persecution, "When they bring you to the synagogue and magistrates and authorities, do not worry about how or what you should answer, or what you should say, for the Holy Spirit will teach you I that very hour what you ought to say" (Luke 12:11-12). The apostle Paul spoke of "the sword of the Spirit, which is the word of God," and invoked prayer "that utterance may be given to me, that I may open my mouth boldly to make known the mystery of the gospel, for which I am an ambassador in chains; that in it I may speak boldly as I ought to speak" (Ephesians 6:17-20). The prophet

Isaiah testified, "The Lord God has given me the tongue of the learned, that I should know how to speak a word in season to him who is weary" (Isaiah 50:4).

The Holy Spirit will *convict of sin, righteousness, and judgment.* "And when He has come, He will convict the world of sin, and of righteousness, and of judgment: of sin because they do not believe in Me; of righteousness because I go to the Father and you see me no more; of judgment because the ruler of this world is judged" (John 16:8-11). The Holy Spirit convicts or convinces the world of the seriousness of sin, the possibility of righteousness, and the inevitability of judgment. To accomplish this conviction, He brings forth evidence.

He uses unbelief to convict the world of sin. Jesus said, "Because they do not believe in me." Unbelief is the root of all other sins (see Romans 14:23). Unbelief is a rejection of God's way and makes Him a liar. Unbelief is living your life in self-centered independence, disowning any reliance on God. Unbelief is not an intellectual problem; it is a moral problem. It doesn't come from the head but from the heart (Hebrews 3:12).

The Holy Spirit uses the victory of Jesus Christ to convict the world of the possibility of righteousness. Jesus said, "Because I go to My Father and you see Me no more." His return to the Father was through His resurrection and ascension, events that proved that His sin-bearing death was a finished and satisfactory work, thus providing for our justification (see 2 Corinthians 5:21).

The Spirit uses the devil's defeat to prove to the world the inevitability of judgment. Jesus said, "Because the ruler of this world is judged." By His death, resurrection, and ascension, Jesus won a decisive victory over the devil. If the ruler of the world has been judged, then the world that he rules will also be judged.

Sin, righteousness, and judgment become solemn realities only by the convicting work of the Holy Spirit.

The Fatherhood of God

At the heart of the Kingdom is a Father. Jesus brought an entirely new picture of God into the world. The Jews had no concept of God as One with whom they could have an intimate personal relationship. God was Father only in the sense that the nation of Israel as a corporate whole was His son. In other words, sonship was national rather than individual. Jews of the first century with their transcendental view of God could not conceive that He could be thought of in terms of intimate fellowship. God was too far removed and too holy to approach except with the morning and evening sacrifices offered daily in the temple at Jerusalem. God was the judge of all humankind, and He was tough and harsh in His demands. People accustomed to approaching God with holy fear were shocked at the teaching of Jesus that you could use the name *Abba* in a relationship with God. The word means "Daddy." It was the intimate family word that a child used for his dad. In all the history of Israel, no one had used this word in reference to God. It was unthinkable, yet Jesus confidently referred to God by this intimate family name. The most astounding thing is that He told His followers that they could also call God *Abba*, meaning that our relationship with God was like son to father. God is a loving Father who extends His mercy to us who don't deserve it. Jesus taught in Matthew 6 that God is a benevolent Father who cares for our needs. Furthermore, according to Luke 15, God the Father not only welcomes the repentant sinner when he returns but goes out to seek him. Jesus showed us that as Father there is nothing God wants more than to embrace us and welcome us home. Jesus also emphasized the righteousness and holiness of God. He did not come to found a new religion based on the performance of religious duties. He called for righteousness that went deeper than ceremonial conformity. It was holiness that was based upon the nature of God, to "be perfect, just as your Father in heaven is perfect" (Matthew 5:48).

The Primacy of Love

It's abundantly clear that the teachings of Jesus were revolutionary, so much so that they goaded the religious authorities to hound Him to death. One feature of His teachings that was particularly offensive to them was to de-emphasize the importance of outward ceremonial displays of religion and stress the inner condition of the heart. Three things dominated Judaism in the first century. The first was the temple, with its endless ritual sacrifices. The second was the Sabbath, with an overwhelming burden of prohibitions imposed upon it by extreme legalism. The third was the Law of God, not as it was originally written and intended in the Old Testament, but as it was interpreted by the religious authorities. The oral law, that is, the interpretation of the written law in minute detail by the authoritative teachers, was just as binding as the Law itself. Therefore, righteousness consisted of rigidly participating in the festivals and sacrifices at the temple, keeping the Sabbath holy according to the standards of the Pharisees, and obeying the oral law meticulously. It was all a matter of doing, doing, doing.

Jesus changed this concept of righteousness. God does not want servants dutifully performing religious rituals. Going through the forms of religion does not bring one into the Kingdom of God. He wants sons and daughters who enjoy a loving filial relationship with Him. As far as the temple was concerned, Jesus taught in John 4:21-24 that God is Spirit, and as such He is present everywhere and not confined to places. Therefore, He can be worshiped anywhere. In addition, Jesus declared that One greater than the temple was among them (Matthew 12:6).

Furthermore, He announced that He was Lord of the Sabbath and that the Sabbath was made for man, meant to be a blessing not a burden to those who observe it (Matthew 12:8; Mark 2:27). He repeatedly healed on the Sabbath, demonstrating that "it is lawful to do good on the Sabbath" (Matthew 12:12). Concerning the Law, Jesus taught that "the first and great commandment" is to "love the Lord your God with all your heart, with all your soul, and with all your mind. And the second is like it: You shall love your neighbor as yourself" (Matthew 22:36-40). He even had the audacity to say to pious patriotic Jews that they should love their enemies (Matthew 5:44). The last commandment He gave to His followers before His betrayal was, "Love one another, as I have loved you, that you also love one another. By this all will know that you are My disciples, if you have love for one another."

The biblical word for "love" is *agape*, and Jesus introduced the true meaning of the word. Apart from about 20 uses of the word in the Greek translation of the Old Testament, the word was practically non-existent in secular Greek before the New Testament. Ordinary people of the world didn't like the word *agape*, because to them it bespoke of a servile, cowardly quality. Yet, the fact that "God so *loved* the world that He gave His only begotten Son" for us casts an entirely new light on love. The word means total self-giving for the totally unworthy. That's what God the Father did for us. That's what Jesus embodied. That's what He commanded His followers to do. You will find a lengthy exposition of this command of Jesus in my volume *Kingdom Community.*

The Authority of the King's Teaching

Several times we read that people were awestruck by the teachings of Jesus that displayed His insightful wisdom (Matthew 22:22), His profound interpretation of the Old Testament (Matthew 22:33), and His evident authority, which they contrasted with the teachings of the scribes, who were the professional teachers of the Law (Matthew 7:28-29; Mark 1:21-22). Since the scribes were experts in the Old Testament Law, the people regarded their Scriptural interpretations as binding. The scribes customarily taught by citing the opinions of various rabbis on different matters, appealing not to their own authority but to the authority of others. Jesus, however, in instructing the people appealed to only one authority, and that was to the authority of the Father (John 12:49-50). He knew the mind of God, and the Father commissioned Him to speak it. The entire Sermon on the Mount (Matthew 5-7) illustrates Christ's authority with the repeated statement, "You have heard that it was said . . . but *I say to you . . ..*" In Greek grammar, the word "I" is used in the most emphatic way possible. Jesus contrasted His understanding of the Old Testament Scriptures with the understanding of the scribes. He did not rely on the expertise of others, nor did He quote their teachings as binding. He made it clear that His teaching superseded theirs. In fact, as we have seen, He spoke with the very words of God the Father.

THE DEEDS OF THE KING

"The Kingdom of God is not in word but in power," and the gospel does "not come to you in word only, but also in power" (1 Corinthians 4:20; 1 Thessalonians 1:5). The Book of Acts abundantly demonstrates the reality of those statements. Regrettably, the opposite is more frequently true of contemporary expressions of the gospel: "The Kingdom of God does not consist in power but in talk."

It would have accomplished little if Jesus had only *talked* about the Kingdom but didn't *do* anything about it. He did more than simply proclaim the arrival of the sovereign rule of God. He came to apply it directly to our everyday lives. He came on a search and rescue mission "to seek and to save that which was lost" (Luke 19:10). He came to bring healing and salvation to a sinful people "having no hope and without God in the world" (Ephesians 2:12). He was so effective in His mission that huge crowds followed Him to hear His words, observe His works, and receive the benefits He offered to ordinary people in need.

Signs and Wonders

We have already discussed the miracles of Jesus as proclamations of the Kingdom of God. Therefore, we will simply present a brief review of their significance. His miracles were all implicit claims to His deity, anticipated in the prophecies of the Old Testament: "Behold, your God will come . . . and save you. Then the eyes of the blind shall be opened, and the ears of the deaf shall be unstopped. Then the lame shall leap like a deer, and the tongue of the dumb sing" (Isaiah 35:4-6). Those things happened during the ministry of Jesus. They are not fairy tales or conjuring tricks. His miracles are clear pointers to the reality that He is God in their midst. Scholars throughout the centuries have tried without success to discredit the miracles as fables. This is not the place to refute their efforts or to cite evidence of the trustworthiness of the biblical accounts. It's sufficient to say that there is irrefutable contemporary evidence, both from the followers of Jesus and His opponents. The disciples were clear about His miracles. The Jewish authorities could not deny their reality, so they attributed them to the power of the devil. One of the earliest non-biblical supportive references to the miracles is from a fascinating letter written in A.D. 124. It was written by a Christian apologist named Quadratus to convince the Roman emperor Hadrian of the truth of Christianity:

> But the works of our Savior were always present (for they were genuine): namely those who were healed, those who rose from the dead. They were not only seen in the act of being healed or raised, but they remained always present. And not merely when the Savior was on earth, but after His departure as well. They lived on for a considerable time, so much so that some of them have survived to our own day.

> The miracles began at the birth of Jesus, without a human father. They continued throughout His ministry--miracles of healing and exorcism, nature miracles (such as feeding the multitude, stilling the storm, walking on water), and raising the dead. The

supreme miracle, of course, was His own resurrection from the grave. The miracles of Jesus reveal a God who cares. Everywhere Jesus went, He demonstrated divine compassion, and there is no record that He sent anyone away unsatisfied.

The response that Jesus gave to John's question tells us a lot about the purpose of His miracles (Luke 7:22). They are the fulfillment of prophecies, a sign that Jesus is the long-awaited Messiah. They are a sign of His authority, His power, and His glory. They are a sign of God's love for us and that we can trust Him.

As indicated by the contemporary responses to the miracles, they present an inescapable challenge. If you see somebody who has been undeniably dead for four days walk out of the tomb, you must decide about the one responsible. Is He, or is He not, what He claims to be? Has He, or Has He not, brought the Kingdom of God with power? You cannot ignore the significance of the miracles of Jesus, because they are the key to what He did. Almost everything He did included the demonstration of miraculous powers. With Him arrived the Kingdom of God, and it could not be hidden. This activity of Jesus resulted in a twofold effect. Some who heard His teachings and observed His power answered His call to follow Him. Others, however, already had their minds made up. Jesus had no formal theological training, nor was He ordained. There was a problem, however. The miracles were observable and thus undeniable, so what was the source of His power? Obviously, there was only one conclusion. Satan was the authority behind Him.

We face the same decision. We can try to give a naturalistic explanation of the miracles, but that has been tried many times and failed every time. We can brand Him a fraud, but there is no evidence of such. We can admit that the miracles happened, but it was the devil's power that brought them about. Or we can make the confession, "My Lord and My God!" One thing is certain, and it's that we must make up our minds. We cannot sit on the fence forever.

The Radical Kingdom Perspective

Jesus challenged Jewish tradition not only in His teachings but in His behavior. The Kingdom of God has a different value system that challenges the world's standards. I have chosen one incident in the social life of Jesus to illustrate the radical change that the Kingdom of God makes in our attitudes. Luke 14 tells of a meal that Jesus attended at the invitation of a prominent Pharisee. The context of the situation reveals that likely it was deliberately arranged to entrap Jesus. In verse 1 we read that "they watched Him closely," as though they were waiting for the moment for Jesus to commit some wrongdoing, like what they had done in Mark 3:2 and Luke 6:8-11. They weren't watching to see if He used His knife and fork correctly, but something more significant. It was the Sabbath, and something was going to happen that would test the attitude of Jesus concerning the Law. So, there was an icy and suspicious atmosphere as the meal began.

Suddenly, there was an inconvenient and embarrassing intrusion into the polite social event. A man with dropsy appeared before them. It was unlikely that he could have gotten in by legitimate means, which gives credence to the likelihood of a set-up. The presence of this diseased man would render the meal contaminated and defiled, and the guests would have to go through ritual cleansing before they could continue the meal. How would Jesus handle the situation?

Here is the scene: It was the Sabbath. Work was not permitted on the Sabbath, and healing was work. Jesus had the power to heal, so would He defy Sabbath law by healing the man with dropsy? The scheme of the Pharisees to trap Jesus fails. Although Jesus was "Lord of the Sabbath" (Luke 6:5), He never subverted the Law in its true intent.

He circumvented the senseless legalistic interpretations of the Law which enslave people. Challenged by confrontation with this defiled, unclean man, Jesus disregarded contamination by touching him and healing him.

The Kingdom of God is about healing the untouchable. Having touched and healed the man, Jesus "let him go," a word that means "to set free" or "to liberate." The Kingdom of God is about liberating those who are enslaved through the saving act of Jesus. It is not about futile rules and regulations and legalism and judging what might be right or wrong on the Sabbath. Entering the Kingdom of God brings liberation.

There is irony in what happened next at the meal. The chapter begins by saying, "They watched Him closely," but verse 7 tells us that He was watching them. He saw their normal, routine behavior in grabbing the best seats, the places of honor. Then He taught the lesson that *the Kingdom of God is about doing the unreasonable.* People of the world are taught to look out for themselves, to seek recognition, to chase after positions of honor and prestige, to enjoy the adulation of others. But Jesus taught that the way of the Kingdom is to set aside the normal, social, conventional behavior and take the lowest place genuinely, with integrity. In fact, Kingdom citizens are so busy waiting on tables that they don't have time to sit down. Their occupation is serving, not seat picking.

Beginning in Luke 14:12, Jesus turned to address the man who had invited Him. In Jewish society, you didn't invite people who were beneath your level. Besides your friends and relatives, you would invite rich, significant people who would bring you prestige and higher social standing by their presence. You would invite people who would return the favor by inviting you to their party. If this practice sounds familiar, it's probably because that's exactly what happens today. We grade people according to their usefulness to us. But the Kingdom of God is upside down from the kingdom of the world. While the world values people who are rich, beautiful, and powerful, the Kingdom of God is more concerned with spiritual standards. Jesus said, "The last will be first, and the first last" (Matthew 20:16). *The Kingdom of God is about inviting the undesirable.* The Kingdom principle is to invite those who are not able to invite us back and unable to repay us, like those that are listed in Luke 14:13. The world's motive is to give in order to control or at least to get something in return. But the Kingdom principle is to give with no strings attached and no return expected. Jesus said that giving for the sheer joy of giving leads to a state of blessedness and future reward (verse 14). In the Kingdom of God, His grace at work in our lives causes us to flow out with love into the lives of others.

Verse 15 describes one guest at the meal who was so excited at the teaching of Jesus that he was confident of a seat at the Messianic banquet that takes place at the end of the age (see Isaiah 25:6-9; Luke 22:16; Revelation 19:9). In a parable Jesus taught that *the Kingdom of God excludes those who reject God's invitation of grace but includes those who are unworthy but who accept in faith God's invitation.* Those respectable people that you would expect to be included forfeited their opportunity, but others who felt so undeserving that they had to be coaxed into coming will be found at the King's banquet.

At this meal, Jesus exposed the sins of hard-heartedness, pride, disobedience, and rejection. It's quite clear that the Kingdom of God operates in a way that is entirely different from the world's conventional behavior.

THE DEATH OF THE KING

It is no exaggeration to say that Jesus lived in order to die. His death, in His own language, was the "hour" for which He had come into the world and toward which He was steadily and deliberately moving (John 12:27). When on His last evening He instituted a supper by which His followers were to commemorate Him, He gave them bread to eat and wine to drink, which spoke to them not of His birth, nor His life, nor His teaching, nor His miracles, but of His violent death on the cross. The cross is central to the gospel message, and from the beginning, it has been the symbol of the Christian faith.

The Old Testament anticipates the death of Jesus typically in its many offerings and sacrifices and prophetically in its explicit pronouncements, as in Psalm 22 and Isaiah 53. Of the 89 chapters in the four Gospels, 25 ½ are about the last week of Jesus' life. More than a third of the entire record is devoted to one week in a life of more than 30 years. Paul declared that when he came to Corinth, he decided to know nothing among them except Christ and Him crucified (1 Corinthians 2:2). He also said that he considered as of first importance the fact that Christ died for our sins according to the Scriptures (1 Corinthians 15:3). The rest of the New Testament gives the same emphasis on the death of Christ.

Throughout the Bible, from the early chapters of Genesis to the final chapters of Revelation, you can trace a scarlet thread. The cross has never been a popular message, simply because God's plan of redemption strikes a blow at man's pride. People want to know God intellectually and don't want to admit their helplessness as sinners. But God has decreed that people will be saved by the cross, not by their own wisdom. They must humble themselves to believe, that is, to accept the benefit of the cross as a free and unmerited gift. The Bible describes the reactions to the preaching of the cross among Jews and Greeks (1 Corinthians 1:18-23). The Jews looked for powerful signs, so the message of a supposed Messiah who was crucified in weakness was a stumbling block to them. The Greeks, however, had a passion for wisdom. They imagined that they could attain knowledge of God by their intellect and reason, so the cross to them was foolishness.

The cross is still a stumbling block to agnostics who demand signs and specify the conditions upon which they are prepared to believe. It is a stumbling block to the self-righteous who refuse to humble themselves to accept salvation as a free gift. And the cross is foolishness to intellectuals who ridicule its message as a hangover from primitive and superstitious blood rituals. But to those who are saved, the cross is "the power of God and the wisdom of God" (1 Corinthians 1:24).

His Death Was Inevitable

Jesus repeatedly insisted during His public ministry that He must suffer and die. He never spoke of His sufferings and forthcoming death in a doubtful or undetermined manner but in definite and clear terms. In announcing His death, He used a verb translated as "must," signifying something that was inevitable and necessary (Matthew 16:21; Mark 8:32; Luke 9:22; 17:25; 24:7, 26; John 3:14). The death of Jesus was inevitable because of several reasons. From a divine viewpoint, it was a necessary part of God's plan of salvation, as seen in the statements of Jesus announcing His death. Christ's death was the predetermined counsel of God. His sufferings, death, and resurrection must all come to pass because of the immutable decree of God, and in line with the covenant of grace. Had He not died to pay the penalty for our sins, there would be no hope of forgiveness, because there would never be another offering suitable enough. We will enlarge this feature of His death later.

There are at least two earthly factors that suggest the inevitability of Christ's death. First, there is an ugly quality of human nature that is threatened by decency and goodness. The moral perfection of Jesus was the greatest threat to this dark side of human nature. Jesus gives the explanation in John 3:19-20: "And this is the condemnation, that the light has come into the world, and men loved darkness rather than light, because their deeds were evil. For everyone practicing evil hates the light and does not come to the light, lest his deeds should be exposed."

The other reason is the irrevocable conflict between Jesus and the Jewish religious leaders. His entire ministry brought embarrassment to them, with resulting rage. His teachings concerning the Law totally opposed their legalistic interpretations and exposed their hypocrisy. His disregard for their inane regulations pertaining to the Sabbath was infuriating. His association with the dregs of society and non-Jews was scandalizing. They could explain His undeniable miracles only by attributing them to the power of the devil. It's no wonder that very early in the ministry of Jesus there was a coalition of various factions of Jewish leadership that plotted the death of Jesus (Mark 3:6).

His Death Was Voluntary

We have seen that God the Father sent His Son into this world on a rescue mission, one that necessitated His death. Jesus pursued His entire ministry in the consciousness of the fact that it would lead to a dreadful end, yet He obeyed. There was never the slightest deviation from the appointed pathway. He said, "I have come down from heaven, not to do My own will, but the will of Him who sent Me" (John 6:38). That obedience led Him "to the point of death, even the death of the cross" (Philippians 2:8). Christ accepted death as the issue of His life on earth, and He lived with a sense of compulsion concerning His death, as revealed in the repeated announcements that His death was necessary. A well-known painting by Holman Hunt, entitled "The Shadow of Death," depicts Jesus as a boy standing with outstretched arms before an open window in the carpenter's shop in Nazareth. The sunlight streaming through the window casts His shadow in the form of a cross on the wall behind Him, where the tool rack looks like a horizontal bar on which His hands have been crucified. To one side kneels His mother among the wood chippings. She looks startled, as though she has a preview of the tragic scene that is to come.

Jesus made no efforts to protect Himself from death. On the night that He was arrested in Gethsemane, He told the only one of His followers who was armed to put away his weapon, explaining that He could call on more than 72,000 angels to defend Him (Matthew 26:52-53). Instead of offering a defense at His trial, He remained silent even though He knew that the charges against Him were baseless (Matthew 27:12-14). When the Roman governor boasted that he had the authority to crucify Jesus or release Him, Jesus responded that he would have no power whatsoever over Him unless God allowed it (John 19:10-11).

Jesus had already declared that nobody could take His life, because only He had the power to lay His life down and to take it up again (John 10:17-18). In earthly kingdoms, they do everything possible to keep the king alive, because worldly kingdoms depend upon the king's survival. But the Kingdom of God, which is not of this world

(John 18:36), will only survive and thrive if the King dies.

His Death Was Substitutionary

Why did Jesus have to die? What's the meaning of the cross? Without using a lot of academic and theological jargon, let me attempt to summarize as simply as possible the meaning of the death of Jesus. Some teach that the purpose of the death of Jesus was to prove that God's love is inextinguishable and inexhaustible, and that is certainly true. Romans 5:8 declares, "God demonstrates His own love toward us, in that while we were still sinners, Christ died for us."

Others teach that Jesus died to set an everlasting example of how to bear undeserved suffering with bravery and patience, and that is true. To encourage believers who were being persecuted for the sake of Jesus, Peter pointed them to the sinless Jesus who suffered for them and left them an example to follow (1 Peter 2:19-23).

But the death of Jesus is much more than a demonstration of love and an inspiring example of patient fortitude. If that's all His death involved, how do we explain expressions like redemption and the forgiveness of sins? How can we explain the dreadful agony of Jesus in the garden as the cross approached? Did He face physical pain and death with less courage than countless martyrs? If Christ died only as an example of love and undeserved suffering, human needs would still be unmet. We need more than an example; we need a Savior.

The Bible explains the death of Jesus by connecting it with our sins. God is a holy God. That means that God is infinitely righteous and just, and as such He has a burning hatred for sin. By contrast, we are sinful—sinful by birth, by nature, by choice, and by practice. A holy God cannot overlook sin. He has said, "The wages of sin is death" (Romans 6:23) and "The soul who sins shall die" (Ezekiel 18:20). We are hell-deserving sinners, and we rightfully deserve to die an eternal death. God would no longer be holy and just if He disregarded His own law and overlooked sin. All sin will be punished, but the question is, "Who will bear that punishment?" The answer is that either you will bear it or Christ bears it for you. Your sin will be pardoned in Christ or punished in hell, but it will never be overlooked.

In Exodus 12 we read about the Passover lamb that was a substitute for the first-born male among the Hebrews in Egypt. It was a picture and a prophecy of the substitutionary death of Jesus Christ. The Bible says that we are redeemed "with the precious blood of Christ, as of a lamb without blemish and without spot" (1 Peter 1:18-19). In the pages of the New Testament, we find the recurring statement, "Christ died for our sins (1 Corinthians 15:3; 1 Peter 3:18; 1 John 3:5). Several words descriptive of the death of Jesus are important at this point. The word *redemption* signifies a price paid to buy back something. Through the blood of Christ, we are redeemed from the guilt, the penalty, the power, and the consequences of sin (1 Peter 1:18-19; Hebrews 9:12). *Justification* is a legal term that declares the sinner not guilty because Christ has borne for him the punishment for sin and has met the demands of the Law (Romans 5:9). *Reconciliation* and its synonym, *atonement*, denote the making of peace between two parties previously at variance. Sin estranged us from God; the cross brought atonement. Sin caused enmity with God; the cross brought peace. Sin created a chasm between man and God; the cross bridged it. Sin broke our fellowship with God; the cross restored it.

The Bible says, "God was in Christ reconciling the world to Himself, not imputing their trespasses to them" (2 Corinthians 5:19). If God doesn't count our sins against us, what does He do with them? We have already seen that He doesn't overlook them. He puts them on Christ instead (2 Corinthians 5:21). He made Christ to be sin for us.

Christ was sinless in every respect, with no sins of nature, thought, word, or deed. But God laid our sins on Him, and they defiled Him. He "bore our sins in His own body on the tree" (1 Peter 2:24). He endured their penalty, which is death. That's wonderful news, but there is still more. When our sins are laid on Christ, through faith His righteousness is laid on us (1 Peter. 2:24; 2 Corinthians 5:21). He was made sin with our sins that we might become righteous with His righteousness! Here is the unfathomable purpose of God in the death of Jesus. That death satisfied both the justice and the love of God, and it reconciles sinners unto God.

His Death Was Sufficient

God's purpose for the death of Jesus was fulfilled. "For Christ also suffered once for sins, the just for the unjust, that He might bring us to God" (1 Peter 3:18). "When we were enemies we were reconciled to God through the death of His Son" (Romans 5:10). Sin separated us from God, but on the cross, Jesus paid the sin debt that He might bring us to God. The Greek word for "bring" is the word used to introduce someone to an important potentate, such as a king. To get to God, you must go through Jesus.

Notice in 1 Peter 3:18 that Jesus suffered *once* for sins (see Hebrews 10:10). That word "once" doesn't mean once upon a time. It means once and for all, never to be repeated. When Jesus died upon the cross, the sin debt was fully paid. God's justice was absolutely satisfied. Just before He died, Jesus said, "It is finished" (John 19:30). Those words translate one Greek word, *tetelestai*, which may be translated as "paid in full." Jesus carried out sins to the cross and paid our debt in full. He successfully finished the mission for which He was sent to accomplish.

THE VICTORY OF THE KING

The crucifixion of Jesus was the darkest day of all history. The forlorn words of the two disciples on the road to the village of Emmaus three days later summarize the despondency of those who had proclaimed the deity of Jesus: "We were hoping that it was He who was going to redeem Israel" (Luke 24:21). The death of the one they had proclaimed King crushed all their hopes and expectations. Jesus chided them for their weak faith and dullness of understanding the Scriptures and asked, "Ought not the Christ to have suffered these things and to enter into His glory (Luke 24:25-26). Then He proceeded to teach them all the Old Testament prophecies concerning Himself.

The gospel story did not end with the death of Christ. The might of God's power "was worked in Christ when He raised Him from the dead" (Ephesians 1:20), and beyond the resurrection lies the exaltation of Jesus to the right hand of God and His enthronement and glorification in heaven.

The Resurrection of the King

The apostle Paul, testifying to King Agrippa concerning Jesus, asked, "Why should it be thought incredible by you that God raises the dead?"

(Acts 26:8). That question concerning the Resurrection of Jesus rests on a solid foundation because that event is the best-authenticated fact in all history. Luke wrote that Jesus "presented Himself alive after His suffering by many infallible proofs" (Acts 1:3). The term "infallible proofs" translates a Greek word (*tekmeriois*) used only this one time in the Bible. It literally means "many criteria of certainty," and in secular Greek, it designated irrefutable evidence, the strongest proof possible. Luke was referring to the testimony of people who knew beyond all doubt that Jesus Christ had risen bodily from the tomb. The Bible records at least eleven occasions on which Jesus appeared to people during the 40 days following His Resurrection. They saw Him, touched Him, spoke with Him, and ate with Him. He appeared both to individuals and to groups, on one occasion to more than 500 people (1 Corinthians 15:6). The apostle John was privileged to see Jesus not only in His resurrection body but also in His glorified body (Revelation 1:18). Saul of Tarsus also saw Jesus in His glorified state (Acts 9:3-6; 22:6-11; 26:13-18). No wonder the apostle Peter wrote, "We did not follow cunningly devised fables when we made known to you the power and coming of our Lord Jesus Christ, but were eyewitnesses of His majesty" (2 Peter 1:16).

Many volumes have been published setting forth the overwhelming evidence concerning the Resurrection of Jesus, and you can examine the evidence for yourself. I will mention only two volumes. In the early part of the eighteenth century, two able young men, Gilbert West and George Lord Lyttleton, both professed deists, went to Oxford determined to attack the very basis of the Christian faith. Their credentials were impressive. Both were lawyers who swam in the mainstream of English society, and Lyttleton, in addition to having served as Chancellor of the Exchequer, was a brilliant literary man. In their attempt to administer a death blow to Christianity, Lyttleton settled down to prove that the alleged conversion of Saul of Tarsus was a fraud, while West sought to prove that the Resurrection of Christ never occurred.

Being lawyers, and well-trained in the weighing of evidence, they found to their astonishment that the evidence concerning the Resurrection of Christ unassailable and concerning the conversion of Paul manifestly true. Both men became Christians and published books strongly affirming the biblical accounts of the events they originally sought to disprove. On the fly-leaf of West's book, published in 1747 under the title *Observations on the History and Evidences of the Resurrection of Jesus Christ*, is this quotation: "Blame not before thou has examined the truth."

Frank Morison, an investigative journalist, was a skeptic who was determined to prove that the Resurrection of Jesus was a myth. However, his investigations led him to discover the validity of the biblical account in a moving, personal way. He did write his book, but not the way he originally intended. Instead of attacking the veracity of the story of the Resurrection, his book, published in 1930 with the title *Who Moved the Stone*, is one of the most convincing apologetics ever written supporting the Resurrection.

As we have seen, Jesus made some astounding claims about Himself, including the fact that He would rise from the dead. If He didn't rise from the dead, we have no reason to believe anything He said, including His promise of the forgiveness of sin and eternal life to anyone who believed in Him. He also promised that He would return and create a new heaven and earth. If He never rose from the dead, then He was one of the most consummate blasphemers and liars the world has ever known.

Furthermore, if Jesus did not rise from the dead, the apostles were liars, because they openly proclaimed that He was alive. They risked everything, including their own lives, in continuing to make that proclamation. Would they be willing to die for something that they knew wasn't true? Few people will die for something they know is a lie. All the apostles were persecuted and tortured, and they died as martyrs. People tell lies to get out of trouble. They don't tell lies to get into trouble.

If Jesus had not risen from the dead, the Christian faith simply wouldn't exist. Unlike all other religions, which can survive after the founder dies, Christianity depends on Jesus being alive. Everything hinges on the Resurrection. If Jesus rose from the dead, then you must accept everything else He said as true. If Jesus isn't alive, then He was a deceiver, and you can disregard every claim He made. The decision is yours. You can say that Jesus is a liar, a lunatic, or the Lord.

In his book *Mere Christianity*, C.S. Lewis wrote:

I am trying here to prevent anyone saying the really foolish thing that people often say about Him: "I'm ready to accept Jesus as a great moral teacher, but I don't accept his claim to be God." That is the one thing we must not say. A man who was merely a man and said the sort of things Jesus said would not be a great moral teacher. He would either be a lunatic—on the level with the man who says he is a poached egg—or else he would be the Devil of Hell. You must make your choice. Either this man was, and is, the Son of God, or else a madman or something worse. You can shut him up for a fool, you can spit at him and kill him as a demon or you can fall at his feet and call Him Lord and God, but let us not come with any patronizing nonsense about his being a great human teacher.

The Ascension of the King

We have seen how Jesus Christ renounced the royalties of heaven to come to the poverty of Earth and to take humanity upon Himself for our sake. We have observed that His condescension took Him all the way to death on the cross. We have also seen that death was followed by resurrection. But there is more: "Therefore God also has highly exalted Him and given Him the name which is above every name, that at the name of Jesus every knee should bow, of those in heaven, and of those on earth, and of those under the earth, and that every tongue should confess that Jesus Christ is Lord, to the glory of God the Father (Philippians 2:9-11).

A key word in that passage is the first word, "therefore," which draws a consequence from what is written immediately before, that is, concerning the redemptive work of Jesus. He was always Lord, but His lordship has taken on greater dimensions and deeper significance because of His humiliation and crucifixion. In other words, He has greater glory than ever before. In fact, the term "highly exalted" is the translation of a word that is literally "hyper-exalted." It means to go as high as you can possibly go and then go beyond that. Jesus is now Lord in some sense that would never have been possible had He not come to Earth to die for us.

The avenue that brought Him to His exalted state was His ascension, which He Himself predicted in such places as John 6:62 and 20:17, and which is described in Mark 16:19 and Luke 24:51, but most vividly in Acts 1:9-11. If you want to read about the joyful welcome the Lord received when He ascended to heaven, look at Psalm 24:7-10.

The ascension *made effective the Resurrection.* If Christ had been compelled to submit to death again after His resurrection, could we believe that He was the divine giver of life? Could He have bestowed everlasting life and yet Himself have died? Could He have taken victory from the grave and yet have lain in it for centuries? Could He have provided permanent atonement if the sacrifice was only temporarily accepted? All that the resurrection of Jesus means was certified by His ascension. Here is the guarantee that the work He came to do is well done and finished. From the cross, Jesus said, "*It* is finished," not "*I* am finished."

The ascension was the *completion of all that was involved in the incarnation.* Jesus became man when He came to Earth, and He did so without giving up His deity. It's important to realize that He did not discard His humanity when He died on the cross or when He rose from the dead. It was still as man that He rose victorious over sin and death, and it was still as man that He ascended to the Father. Rather than laying aside His humanity at His exaltation, Christ retained it, so that He might exercise on our behalf His high priestly ministry. Thus, the Bible could speak of "Christ who died, and furthermore is also risen, who is even at the right hand of God, who also makes intercession for us" (Romans 8:34), and also declare that the great High Priest in heaven who can sympathize with our weaknesses is the same Jesus who "was in all points tempted as we are" (Hebrews 4:15).

> Though now ascended up on high,
>
> He bends on earth a brother's eye;
>
> Partaker of the human name,
>
> He knows the frailty of our frame.

Our fellow-sufferer yet retains

A fellow-feeling of our pains;

And still remembers, in the skies,

His tears, and agonies, and cries.

--Michael Bruce

The ascension *made possible the fulfillment of Christ's promises.* Having come from heaven, Christ must return to heaven, that He might open its gates to redeemed humanity and then come again to claim His own as He promised (John 14:2). His life above is the promise and guarantee of our own. It was expedient that Jesus return to heaven so that He might be with His followers always and everywhere (Matthew 28:20), and that He might send the Holy Spirit as He promised (John 16:7-14). The Lord's ascension opened for all believers an intimacy and fellowship with God otherwise impossible. Christ became physically remote so that He might become spiritually near, free from earthly limitations.

The Enthronement of the King

Several New Testament passages tell us that following His ascension to heaven, Jesus sat down at the right hand of God. See, for example, Mark 16:19; Acts 2:33; Romans 8:34; Ephesians 1:20; 1 Peter 3:22; and several passages in Hebrews, especially 1:3. The New Testament quotes Psalm 110 more often than any other Old Testament prophecy. The first verse describes the Father enthroning the Son: "The Lord (Jehovah) said to my Lord (Adonai), 'Sit at My right hand, till I make Your enemies Your footstool.'" This is a temporary enthronement, as the word "till" indicates. As we shall see, the day will come when the Lord Jesus Christ arises from the throne of God, take the sword of the conqueror, and come to His own throne. He will then fulfill the promise that He gave in Revelation 3:21: "To him who overcomes, I will grant to sit with Me on My throne, as I also overcame and sat down with my Father on His throne."

Jesus *anticipated His present enthronement* during the shameful injustice of His trial before the Sanhedrin when He declared, "Hereafter you will see the Son of Man sitting at the right hand of the Power" (Matthew 26:64). He knew of His approaching suffering and death, and this was the announcement of His vindication.

The fact that He is at the right hand of God is *proof that He is the eternal Jehovah God.*

For a commentary on that statement, I refer you back to the section "Jesus Is God" in the chapter entitled "Who Is the King?"

His enthronement is *the guarantee that the work He came to do is finished.* The Bible says that Jesus, "when He had by Himself purged our sins, sat down at the right hand of the Majesty on high" (Hebrews 1:3). Later, we are told that Jesus, "after He had offered one sacrifice for sins forever, sat down at the right hand of God" (Hebrews 10:12). His work of redemption was accomplished, and He took His rest. In contrast, in the Old Testament, "every priest stands ministering daily and offering repeatedly the same sacrifices, which can never take away sins" (Hebrews 10:11). In the Tabernacle and later in the Temple, there was not one chair. The priests never sat down, because their work was never done.

His enthronement is *the revelation of our own position with Him.*

Ephesians 1:19-21 speaks of God's "mighty power which He worked in Christ when He raised Him from the dead and seated Him at His right hand in the heavenly places, far above all principality and power and might and dominion and every name that is named, not only in this age but also in that which is to come . . .." I want you now to look closely at Ephesians 2:1, where you will see that the verb is in italics—*He made alive.* That means that those words are not in the Greek text but have been supplied by the translator. Then what did Paul mean if there is no verb in the sentence? He was very fond of parenthetical expressions, which is what we find in Ephesians 2:22-23. In other words, 2:1 is a continuation of 1:21, and the words in italics should not be included. Verse 21 is actually a descriptive statement of "the heavenly places," so to get the fullness of the thought, let's read 1:19-20 and then skip to 2:1. This passage brings together almost the whole Greek vocabulary of power—*dunamis* and *energeian,* both meaning explosive power, and *krates,* the power of ruling. All three words are present in 1:19-20, where Paul prays that we may know "the exceeding greatness of His power (*dunamis*) toward us who believe, according to the working (*energeian*) of His mighty power (*krates*) which He worked in Christ when He raised Him from the dead and seated Him at His right hand in the heavenly places . . . and you who were dead in trespasses and sins." That's exactly what God did. When the Lord Jesus died, those who trust in Him died, and we can say, "I have been crucified with Christ" (Galatians 2:20). When Jesus rose from the dead, God counted us as being raised with Him, and we can say, "If then you were raised with Christ, seek those things which are above, where Christ is, sitting at the right hand of God" (Colossians 3:1). When Christ ascended into heaven and was seated upon the throne of God, He "raised us up together, and made us sit together in the heavenly places in Christ Jesus" (Ephesians 2:6). And that is our status in Christ.

The fact that Christ is at God's right hand tells us that *He occupies the place of universal power.* Jesus anticipated this reward when He assured His disciples, "All authority has been given to Me in heaven and on earth" (Matthew 28:18). Ephesians 1:21-23 reveals the dominion of Christ to be threefold. First, He is Lord of all intelligence. His sovereignty extends over both earthly and spiritual beings. The phrase "far above . . . every name that is named" leaves no doubt concerning the universal scope of Christ's power. It's all-inclusive, signifying everything that can bear a name, not only personalities but principles, forces, and circumstances. His sovereignty is not merely temporary but permanent, "not only in this age but also in that which is to come."

Furthermore, Christ is the ruler of the whole universe. God "put all things under His feet," as prophesied in Psalms 8 and 110 (verse 22). All things, material and moral, angelic and human, visible and invisible, good and bad, present and future, are in His hands.

The third area of the sovereignty of Christ is the Church. God "gave Him to be head over all things to the church, which is His body, the fullness of Him who fills all in all" (verses 22-23;). The head is the seat of will and authority, and the body of Christ is to be obedient to every command of the head. The head is the source and seat of life. There is no life in a decapitated corpse, and the Church has no life apart from Christ. Ephesians 5:29-30 and Colossians 2:19 provide beautiful pictures of the concern of Christ the head for His body. The head is the source of sensation. All feeling comes from the brain and resides in it. Christ feels our pain and sympathizes with our weaknesses (Hebrews 4:15). The head is the seat of power, and Christ is the strength of His people. The head is the seat of thought and intelligence, so Christ is our wisdom, our guide, and our mind. The head is the seat of honor, glory, and beauty, so Jesus Christ is the glory of His people, and to Him alone belong all dominion, praise, and love forever.

The enthronement of Christ *has significant implications for our daily practical living.* It instills within us new ambitions and standards, and we concentrate on those things that please our reigning King, pursuing them with single-minded determination. We follow the admonition of Colossians 3:1: "If then you were raised with Christ, seek those things which are above, where Christ is, sitting at the right hand of God."

The enthronement of Christ *encourages our faith.* We have the assurance that we will share His glory. "When Christ who is our life appears, then you also will appear with Him in glory" (Colossians 3:4). We will be like Him, not as great or glorious, but reigning with Him. According to Revelation 5:10, He has "made us kings and priests to our God; and we shall reign on the earth."

The Present Ministry of the King

Jesus is Prophet, Priest, and King. At His first coming, He functioned as a prophet, one who represents God to the people. At His second coming He will reign as King, ruling over everything. In His present ministry, He functions as a priest, one who represents the people to God. "This hope we have as an anchor of the soul, both sure and steadfast, and which enters the Presence behind the veil, where the forerunner has entered for us, even Jesus, having become High Priest forever according to the order of Melchizedek" (Hebrews 6:19-20).

Hebrews 2:1 speaks of the possibility of drifting away from the faith, but as an anchored ship cannot move, our hope in Christ provides certainty and security, no matter what storms may threaten. The "veil" refers to the veil in the Tabernacle that separated the people of Israel from the presence of God. Levitical priests were the only ones able to pass through the veil to intercede to God on Israel's behalf. Jesus is our priest who enters the true veil in heaven to intercede on our behalf. He is "a merciful and faithful High Priest in things pertaining to God, to make propitiation for the sins of the people" (Hebrews 2:17). When Jesus ascended into heavenly places to act as High Priest forever, He entered as our forerunner so that at the right time we too will be ushered into the holy presence of Almighty God. He also is preparing a place for us (John 14:2). His priesthood is like that of Melchizedek, the king of righteousness and the king of peace (Hebrews 7:1-28). In contrast to the inferior status of the temporary Aaronic priesthood, with its earthly limitations and temporary nature, the priesthood of Jesus is heavenly, superior, and eternal (Hebrews 7:16, 24; 8:1).

He Is Our Mediator

Adam and Eve's rebellion in the Garden of Eden severed the relationship between the Creator and His creation and caused a gulf of separation. Because of the chasm caused by sin, mankind was unable to go directly into God's presence. To approach God, the people required a mediator, which was the role of the priests. They were to bring people closer to God by teaching His law and offering sacrifices on their behalf. Essentially, they were mediators, or go-betweens, who facilitated the relationship between God and the people.

Jesus Christ offered Himself as the perfect once-and-for-all sacrifice for the forgiveness of sin to all who would repent, ending the need for a human priesthood to offer sacrifices. Having given Himself as "a ransom for all," Jesus is our "Mediator between God and men" (1 Timothy 2:5). Additional proof of this truth is found in Hebrews 9:15: "For this reason He is the Mediator of the new covenant, by means of death for the redemption of the transgressions under the first covenant, that those who are called may receive the promise of the eternal inheritance." It is because of our great Mediator that we can stand before God clothed in the righteousness of Christ Himself. He is in heaven "to appear in the presence of God for us" (Hebrews 9:24).

He Is Our Intercessor

Prayer was a major part of the life of Jesus while He was on earth (Luke 6:12). From various references in the Gospels, we know that He spent a great deal of time alone with the Father. For the most part, we don't know what He prayed in private, but there are examples of His intercessory prayers. He prayed for little children (Matthew 19:13). He prayed for Peter's faith to remain strong (Luke 22:32). In His High Priestly Prayer, recorded in John 17, He prayed for His followers and "for those who will believe in Me through their word" (verse 20). One of the most significant features of the present ministry of Jesus is that He "is even at the right hand of God, who also makes intercession for us" (Romans 8:34), and He always lives to make intercession for us (Hebrews 7:25).

He Is Our Advocate

Of great assurance to us is that in His present ministry, Jesus represents us. Christ has entered "into heaven itself, now to appear in the presence of God for us" (Hebrews 9:24). Several passages, such as Revelation 12:10, Job 2:1, and Zechariah 3:1, tell us that we have an accuser, Satan, who brings accusations against us before God, mocking the ones that Jesus bought for His own. But if we have an adversary, we have an Advocate. Advocates are representatives who stand in the place of those who cannot speak for themselves and who plead their case for them. "And if anyone sins, we have an Advocate with the Father, Jesus Christ the righteous" (1 John 2:1). We don't have to worry about Satan's malicious charges against us because the One pleading our case is much more powerful. "Who shall bring a charge against God's elect: It is God who justifies. Who is he who condemns? It is Christ who died, and furthermore is also risen, who is even at the right hand of God, who also makes intercession for us" (Romans 8:33-35). For more comments concerning Jesus as our Advocate, see the section "The Holy Spirit" in the chapter entitled "The Teachings of the King."

He Oversees Churches

We have already seen that in His enthronement, Jesus is sovereign over the Church in a universal sense. This sovereignty also includes a ministry toward local churches. In very vivid language, the first chapter of Revelation records a vision of the apostle John when he was in exile on the island of Patmos. John saw the glorified Christ, dressed in the garb of a high priest, standing among seven golden lampstands. Christ told him that the lampstands symbolized local churches in the Roman province of Asia and proceeded to speak messages for John to deliver to each respective church. It is reasonable to conclude that these historical churches were representative of all churches and that the Lord still has an active concern for each one.

Having been enthroned in heaven, Jesus fulfilled His promise to send the Holy Spirit, whose ministry we have briefly described. In addition to the ministry of the Holy Spirit, we must consider Ephesians 4, which tells of the ascended Lord giving gifts of ministry "for the equipping of the saints for the work of ministry, for the edifying of the body of Christ, till we all come to the unity of the faith and of the knowledge of the Son of God, to a perfect man, to the measure of the stature of the fullness of Christ" (Ephesians 4:12-13).

The Return of the King

Both the Old and New Testaments are full of promises about the return of Jesus Christ. Over 1800 references appear in the Old Testament and seventeen Old Testament books give prominence to this theme. In the 260 chapters of the New Testament, there are more than 300 references to the Lord's return, which amounts to one out of every 30 verses. Twenty-three of the 27 New Testament books refer to this great event. Jesus Himself had much to say about His return. He promised His apostles that He would come again (John 14:3). His return was a prominent theme in His teaching on the Mount of Olives, recorded in Matthew 24-25, where He pointed to a future establishment of God's Kingdom on the earth. He described the manner of His coming as being like the brightness of lightning illuminating the entire sky from the east to the west (Matthew 24:27). He said that He would come with power and great glory and with the sound of a great trumpet that awakens the righteous dead, who are then gathered from the ends of the earth (Matthew 24:30-31). Jesus announced to His disciples that He "will come in the glory of His Father with His angels, and then He will reward each according to his works" (Matthew 16:27).

The return of the Lord will be a literal event and will be just like He went to heaven the first time. After Jesus ascended into heaven, the angels declared to the apostles, "'Men of Galilee, why do you stand gazing up into heaven? This same Jesus, who was taken from you into heaven, will so come in like manner as you saw him go into heaven'" (Acts 1:11). Zechariah 14:4 identifies the location of the Second Coming

as the Mount of Olives. The most detailed description of the Second
Coming is found in Revelation 19:11-16:

> "Now I saw heaven opened, and behold, a white horse. And He
> who sat on him was called Faithful and True, and in righteousness
> He judges and makes war. His eyes were like a flame of fire, and
> on His head were many crowns. He had a name written that no
> one knew except Himself. He was clothed with a robe dipped in
> blood, and His name is called The Word of God. And the armies
> in heaven, clothed in fine linen, white and clean, followed Him
> on white horses. Now out of His mouth goes a sharp sword, that
> with it He should strike the nations. And He Himself will rule
> them with a rod of iron. He Himself treads the winepress of the
> fierceness and wrath of almighty God. And He has on His robe
> and on His thigh a name written: KING OF KINGS AND LORD
> OF LORDS."

The Lord's return will be *visible*. We saw in Acts 1:11 that He
went away literally, actually, bodily, and visibly, and He's coming back
literally, actually, bodily, and visibly. The Bible says, "Behold, He is
coming with clouds, and every eye will see Him" (Revelation 1:7).
The Lord will come *suddenly and swiftly*, like a bolt of lightning (Matthew
24:27). His coming will be like *a thief*, unannounced and catching
some people unprepared and unawares. (Matthew 24:43; Luke 12:39;
1 Thessalonians 5:2; 2 Peter 3:10; Revelation 3:3; 16:15). His coming
will be *glorious* (Matthew 24:20; Titus 2:13). He came first in humble
surroundings. When He comes again, it will be in splendor. At His first
coming, He was despised and rejected. When He comes again, every
knee shall bow before Him. His first coming was for crucifixion. When
He comes again, it will be for coronation. At His first coming, He came to

a tree. When He comes again, He will come to a throne. When He came the first time, they spat upon Him. When He comes again, they will lay crowns at His feet. When the Lord returns, He will come with *vengeance* (2 Thessalonians 1:7-9; Revelation 19:14-16). He will execute judgment on all His enemies.

Truly, the "glorious appearing of our great God and Savior Jesus Christ" is our "blessed hope" (Titus 2:13). It is not our intent to give an intricate account of the events surrounding the Lord's return, only to emphasize that this is the occasion of the culmination of all the prophecies pertaining to the Kingdom of God. At this time the Kingdom of God is invisible, but when Jesus triumphantly returns, He will establish the physical, visible Kingdom of God to rule over the world. At that time, all that was forfeited because of the rebellion in Eden will be restored. King Jesus "shall have dominion also from sea to sea, and from the River to the ends of the earth. Those who dwell in the wilderness will bow before Him. . . .Yes, all kings shall fall down before Him; all nations shall serve Him" (Psalm 72:7-11). Even creation itself will share in that triumph, "for the earnest expectation of the creation eagerly waits for the revealing of the sons of God. For the creation was subjected to futility, not willingly, but because of Him who subjected it in hope; because the creation itself also will be delivered from the bondage of corruption into the liberty of the children of God" (Romans 8:19-21). For more, see Part I, "The Kingdom."

II

Conclusion

The Kingdom of God is an invisible community now. Wherever people are born again and serve Jesus Christ, there is the Kingdom. In that sense, as we have seen, we can regard the Kingdom as having already come. In another sense, as we have also seen, it will come when the Lord returns and makes the Kingdom visible. So, the Kingdom of God is both here and yet to come, that is, in its culmination. When we pray, as Jesus taught us, "Your Kingdom come," we pray for its coming in the conversion of souls and submission to the will of God, but we are also praying for its final coming at the return of the Lord. Many people think of the Kingdom only in terms of the present, and they talk about "bringing in the Kingdom," meaning getting the world saved. But we have concluded, and I think rightly so, that the Bible teaches the visible Kingdom awaits the return of the King.

We may be living in what we call the Kingdom Present, but it's possible even now to enjoy some of the blessings of the Kingdom Future. The Bible speaks of those who have experienced the new birth and received the Holy Spirit tasting "the good word of God and the powers of the age to come" (Hebrews 6:4-5). Fanny Crosby wrote about the assurance of salvation as "a foretaste of glory divine." We experience the taste of that glory by the indwelling of the Holy Spirit, who "is the guarantee (earnest, first installment) of our inheritance" (Ephesians 1:14). We taste those powers when we fellowship with the King through prayer, Bible study, and worship; when we marvel at the wonders of creation; when we hear the melody of a songbird; when we are embraced by the love, comfort, and security of family and home; when we enjoy the camaraderie of close companions; and in myriads of other ways. As the old hymn *Marching to Zion* declares, we can experience the delights of heaven on earth:

> The hill of Zion yields
> A thousand sacred sweets
> Before we reach the heavenly fields,
> Or walk the golden streets.
> --Isaac Watts

It's sad that most Kingdom citizens don't exercise their rights of citizenship as they could and should. It's something like living on crackers and cheese when gourmet meals are available. The King has put at our disposal resources that may be had by simple faith, but because of lack of understanding, lethargy, distrust, or other reasons, people rob themselves of those blessings.

Disciples of Jesus Christ walk through the kingdom of this world as citizens of the Kingdom of God. They are not citizens of Earth trying to get to heaven; they are citizens of heaven making their way through this world. Kingdom citizens belong to what the Bible calls "a holy nation" (1 Peter 2:9), a nation within the nations, which happens to be the only Christian nation on Earth. As pointed out earlier in "Kingdom Standards," Kingdom citizens are different. They interpret the news, weigh values, foster relationships, and make decisions by considering their loyalty to the King of the Kingdom.

Kingdom citizens have always faced the same challenges that Jesus encountered. He was a threat to the established system. His teachings defied everything that was supposed to be politically correct. He exposed the inconsistencies and fallacies of traditional Judaism and the hypocrisy of legalistic religious leaders. He presented the most radical and highest of all ethical standards. Who He was, what He did, and what He taught led to a violent unjust death, and He warned that those who followed Him would face the same hatred. When He called people into the Kingdom, He was calling them to Himself. He was the King, and there was no entering the Kingdom without commitment to Him in unreserved loyalty that meant a willingness to die for Him. His arrival inaugurated the Kingdom of God, but those who wanted to become citizens had to give their oath of unwavering allegiance to Him. He made it crystal clear that our eternal destinies are determined by our decision to follow Him or not, and a decision must be made. Nobody can sit on the fence. You either enter the Kingdom by repentance and faith in Jesus, or you remain outside. The King is also the Judge, and He will preside at the highest court of all at the end of time, and every person who has ever lived will give an account to Him.

Acknowledgements

I want to express my sincere gratitude to the thousands of students who have sat in my classrooms around the globe over more than the past sixty years. Their challenging and probing questions have demanded that I remain a student, always probing deeper into the depths of God's revelation of Himself, His purposes, His works, and His ways—all found in the book that He inspired and transmitted to us.

I am grateful to citizens of the Kingdom of God around the world, particularly those in Asia, who have encouraged me to make many of my teachings available in printed form. I particularly want to emphasize the significance of the ministry of International Christian Mission, based in Singapore. Founded in 1983 by the highly esteemed Christian statesman and businessman Hin Hiong Khoo and his wife Marguerite, this organization has operated on a shoestring budget to provide fundamental theological education and ministerial training to more than 100,000 pastors and other Christian leaders, primarily in rural areas of Southeast Asia. Beginning with what Dr. Khoo called a "Bible School in a Briefcase," ICM presented free of charge a curriculum that covered the basics of Christian theology and practical ministry. The curriculum was enlarged over the years, and today it's known as a "Bible School in an E-Case." Modern technology enables ICM to offer an entire Bible School curricu-

lum using a solar-powered audio and video device smaller than an iP-
hone. I have been associated with this mission since 1991 when I was the
dean of Regent University's School of Divinity. Today I have the distinction of bearing the title of chancellor of ICM's schools. This organization
is worthy of the support of all citizens of the Kingdom, and I encourage
you to participate.

I praise God for the Holy Spirit, the agent of divine revelation, who en-
lightens our understanding of that revelation and brings us to higher
levels of comprehension as we diligently and prayerfully apply ourselves to the study of the Bible.

www.ingramcontent.com/pod-product-compliance
Lightning Source LLC
Chambersburg PA
CBHW050508160726
48003CB00001B/220